PROPOSED REFUGEE ADMISSIONS
FOR
FISCAL YEAR 2015

REPORT TO THE CONGRESS

SUBMITTED ON BEHALF OF
THE PRESIDENT OF THE UNITED STATES
TO THE
COMMITTEES ON THE JUDICIARY
UNITED STATES SENATE
AND
UNITED STATES HOUSE OF REPRESENTATIVES

IN FULFILLMENT OF THE REQUIREMENTS OF
SECTIONS 207(d)(1) and (e)
OF THE
IMMIGRATION AND NATIONALITY ACT

UNITED STATES DEPARTMENT OF STATE
UNITED STATES DEPARTMENT OF HOMELAND SECURITY
UNITED STATES DEPARTMENT OF HEALTH AND HUMAN SERVICES

INTRODUCTION

This *Proposed Refugee Admissions for Fiscal Year 2015: Report to the Congress* is submitted in compliance with Sections 207(d)(1) and (e) of the Immigration and Nationality Act (INA). The Act requires that before the start of the fiscal year and, to the extent possible, at least two weeks prior to consultations on refugee admissions, members of the Committees on the Judiciary of the Senate and the House of Representatives be provided with the following information:

(1) A description of the nature of the refugee situation;

(2) A description of the number and allocation of the refugees to be admitted and an analysis of conditions within the countries from which they came;

(3) A description of the plans for their movement and resettlement and the estimated cost of their movement and resettlement;

(4) An analysis of the anticipated social, economic, and demographic impact of their admission to the United States; [1]

(5) A description of the extent to which other countries will admit and assist in the resettlement of such refugees;

(6) An analysis of the impact of the participation of the United States in the resettlement of such refugees on the foreign policy interests of the United States; and

(7) Such additional information as may be appropriate or requested by such members.

This report contains information as required by Section 602(d) of the International Religious Freedom Act of 1998 (Public Law 105-292, October 27, 1998, 112 Stat. 2787) (IRFA) about religious persecution of refugee populations eligible for consideration for admission to the United States. This report meets the reporting requirements of Section 305(b) of the North Korean Human Rights Act of 2004 (Public Law 108-333, October 18, 2004, 118 Stat. 1287) by providing information about specific measures taken to facilitate access to the United States refugee program for individuals who have fled "countries of particular concern" for violations of religious freedoms, identified pursuant to Section 402(b) of the IRFA.

---

[1] Detailed discussion of the anticipated social and economic impact, including secondary migration, of the admission of refugees to the United States is being provided in the *Report to the Congress* of the Refugee Resettlement Program, Office of Refugee Resettlement, Department of Health and Human Services.

FOREWORD

On World Refugee Day, June 20, both President Obama and Secretary Kerry re-affirmed our nation's commitment to helping refugees and our leading role in providing safe haven. This stance reflects our proud heritage as a land welcoming to immigrants. It also reflects a harsh reality. There are currently more refugees, asylum-seekers, and internally displaced persons than at any time since World War II. While starting life anew in the United States may be daunting, it also offers unparalleled hope. It is a chance not only to escape from violence and persecution but to start again. The assistance the American people provide helps newcomers find their footing and feel a part of their new communities. Refugees add to America's vitality and diversity by making substantial contributions to our economic and cultural life.

Resettlement in a third country is a solution for some of the world's most vulnerable refugees, those who would face real danger if they tried to remain where they are or return to the countries they escaped. As a matter of principle, the USRAP offers resettlement to refugees regardless of their location, national origin, health status, occupational skills, or level of educational attainment.

U.S. Arrivals Remain Strong

Refugee arrivals in FY 2014 will again come close to reaching the President's authorized ceiling of 70,000. Close interagency coordination on security checks helped to make this possible because it allowed us to scrutinize and process referrals more carefully and efficiently. We also helped the UN High Commissioner for Refugees (UNHCR) enhance its capacity to refer refugees for resettlement which in turn helped our program reach its ceiling. We had expected 15,000 refugees to arrive from Africa in 2014 but we are now on pace to exceed that. We will also welcome a large number of Iraqi refugees in 2014. Since 2007, we have resettled more than 105,000 Iraqis, despite the challenges of processing refugees in Iraq and some neighboring countries.

Congolese Resettlement

As the world's leading resettlement country and chair of the Congolese Refugee Core Group, the United States will admit more than 3,000 Congolese refugees in FY 2014. In the coming years that number will rise steadily. We continue to work closely with UNHCR to help it resettle at least 50,000 Congolese worldwide over the next 4-5 years. Most of these refugees are in camps in Uganda, Tanzania, Rwanda, and Burundi, and come originally from the

Kivus or Katanga in the Democratic Republic of the Congo. Domestically, we are chairing a Congolese working group, made up of representatives from state governments, nongovernmental organizations, and international organizations who assist with resettlement. Our goal is to better equip Congolese refugees to be resettled in the U.S., to identify additional resources and to help U.S. communities prepare to accept larger numbers of Congolese.

Syrian Refugees

The refugee crisis caused by the conflict in Syria is the worst the world has witnessed in a generation with more than 2.9 million refugees in the region. More than 9 million people need assistance including 6.5 million displaced inside Syria. The U.S. government is deeply committed to assisting the Syrian people and has provided more than $2 billion in humanitarian assistance since the start of the crisis, more than any other donor. While the vast majority of Syrians would prefer to return home when the conflict ends, we recognize that some remain extremely vulnerable in their country of asylum and would benefit from resettlement. UNHCR has announced that it aims to refer 30,000 Syrian refugees to all resettlement countries by the end of calendar year 2014. Those numbers will likely rise in 2015 and 2016. The United States has received more than 2,500 referrals as of August 2014 and expects thousands more in the remainder of the year. We will begin to welcome those Syrians who are approved for U.S. resettlement to communities across the country in larger numbers in 2015.

Unaccompanied Minors from Central America

The number of unaccompanied children crossing the southwest border has risen exponentially. The Administration is taking a whole of government approach that addresses underlying causes of

"Today I join people around the world in commemorating World Refugee Day. It is an opportunity to honor the resilience of those who flee violence and persecution and the dedication of those who help them.

The forces that shatter communities and uproot their residents are difficult to tame. This year we mark a grim milestone. Over 51 million people are now refugees, asylum seekers, or internally displaced persons, according to the United Nations High Commissioner for Refugees. That is more than at any time since World War II.

The United States provides more humanitarian assistance to refugees than any other nation. In the last year alone, the generosity of the American people, and the dedication of those who deliver food, medicine, shelter, and other emergency assistance, have helped to save hundreds of thousands, perhaps millions of lives.

Our commitment does not end overseas. Some refugees simply cannot return home because the risk of violence and persecution is too great. The U.S. admits more refugees for permanent resettlement than any other nation. Last year nearly 70,000 came to the United States and we expect to bring in the same number this year.

The ordeals refugees survive and the aspirations they hold resonate with us as Americans. This country was built by people who fled oppression and war, leapt at opportunity, and worked day and night to remake themselves in this new land. The refugees who arrive in the United States today continue this tradition, bringing fresh dreams and energy and renewing the qualities that help forge our national identity and make our country strong."

President Barack Obama
June 20, 2014
World Refugee Day

migration relating to economic prosperity, governance, and security. One element in our comprehensive strategy to reduce unlawful and dangerous migration to the United States is the planned establishment of in-country refugee programs for minors in Honduras, El Salvador, and Guatemala. The program would be open to certain qualifying lawfully present relatives in the United States to file for unmarried children under 21 who are still residing in their home country and who are eligible to be admitted to the United States as refugees.

Improvements to Global Resettlement

Our efforts to convince more nations to resettle refugees continue to pay dividends. In recent years, countries without a history of resettling refugees have stepped forward and established programs. The list includes Switzerland, which has announced a regular resettlement program, and Japan, which has announced that its pilot program will become permanent next year. In 2013, a total of 27 countries resettled refugees identified and referred by UNHCR. At least 23 countries have agreed to accept Syrian refugees referred by UNHCR, including a number of countries without regular resettlement programs. They will admit Syrians through a humanitarian admissions program.

For several years the U.S. government has provided targeted financial support to UNHCR. One goal is to expand the resettlement capacity and infrastructure it can make available to all countries running resettlement programs. In the Great Lakes region of Africa in particular we have enabled UNHCR to hire more staff. They in turn have been able to refer more refugees to more countries. We have also funded two new interview facilities that all countries can use to screen refugees from the region. The U.S. chairs the Congolese Core Group, made up of countries that have agreed to resettle Congolese refugees and plays an active role in other core groups tasked with resettling additional high priority populations.

"The dreams refugees harbor have special meaning for Americans. Even before our land was a nation, America was a haven for those seeking freedom from persecution, hunger, oppression, and war. Today, refugees continue to look to America for relief and opportunity. These refugees, many of whom arrive having lost everything, become some of the most resilient, entrepreneurial, and devoted citizens we have.

When I visited the UN's Zaatari refugee camp in Jordan last year, I saw firsthand the value and importance of our work. Hundreds of thousands of Syrians – many women and children – live there in suspended animation, waiting for the opportunity to rebuild their lives. I met with some of the camp's many residents. Their needs were simple: food, shelter, stability. But most of all, they want to live their lives with the dignity and respect that all people deserve.

That's why I'm proud that the United States is the largest donor to humanitarian relief worldwide. Our humanitarian assistance has saved lives and eased suffering for 4.7 million people inside Syria and more than 2.8 million refugees in neighboring countries. We have also recently announced nearly $300 million in additional humanitarian assistance to help the people affected by the conflict in South Sudan. Beyond just dollars and programs, our efforts are assisting millions who have fled conflict and persecution in the Central African Republic, Burma, Afghanistan, and many other places around the world."

Secretary John Kerry
June 20, 2014
World Refugee Day

Reuniting Families

In late 2012, the United States reinstated the Priority Three (P-3) family reunification program for spouses, unmarried children under 21, and parents of persons lawfully admitted to the United States as refugees or asylees. It had been suspended for four years after DNA testing uncovered widespread fraud. Since 2012, we have received more than 2,000 P-3 applications for refugees in 50 countries. We are processing them according to more stringent procedures, including DNA testing to verify parent-child relationships. In some countries relatives must register with UNHCR and/or the host government to obtain permission to exit for third country resettlement. Last year we encountered challenges in a number of processing locations where they did not meet this requirement. Accordingly, we have recently tightened the rules for individuals accepted for P-3 consideration, and in most locations will accept applications only for those who meet all relevant local registration requirements.

Combatting Fraud in the Refugee Admissions Program

In 2014, we took additional measures to protect the refugee admissions program against fraud. The Department of State has established new guidelines for its worldwide network of Resettlement Support Centers to improve the way we screen and train staff and interpreters, control access points, manage electronic data, and communicate with applicants. The U.S. government is also working with UNHCR to safeguard refugee referral data by improving registration procedures and enhancing electronic screening of registration data to detect identity fraud.

Ensuring a Suitable Welcome

In FY 2014, to maintain quality reception and placement services for arriving refugees the Department of State continued to guarantee resettlement agencies a minimum level of funding, even during lulls caused when numbers dip, or referrals are delayed so staff and services will be available when needed. The Department expects to continue this funding mechanism in FY 2015.

Benefits and services for refugees include the Reception and Placement grant provided by the State Department, time-limited assistance programs (up to eight months from arrival) and social service programs (up to five years) funded by the Office of Refugee Resettlement at the Department of Health and Human Services (HHS/ORR). These programs help refugees find employment and become economically self-sufficient. They also encourage social integration. The State Department and HHS/ORR continue to work closely with receiving communities to give stakeholders the tools and information they need so that new arrivals can best benefit from the programs and services that are available to them. Over the past year we have consulted with groups in Arizona, Colorado, Illinois, Maine, New York, Texas, Utah, and Wisconsin. ORR established regional offices in order to increase engagement and consultation with resettlement stakeholders. The Administration will continue to explore ways of sustaining a strong federal-state-community partnership and ensuring that refugees can integrate successfully.

Planning for the Future

As we prepare to bring growing numbers of Congolese and Syrian refugees to the United States, we are simultaneously wrapping up longstanding resettlement programs for Burmese in Thailand and Bhutanese in Nepal. In 2014 we continued to process the cases of the more than 5,000 Burmese in Thailand who submitted expressions of interest in resettlement in 2013. The last several thousand eligible Burmese will arrive in the United States in 2015. In Nepal, we worked with UNHCR to issue a last call for expressions of interest among Priority Two (P-2) eligible Bhutanese. Approximately 3,000 individuals registered their interest by the June 30 deadline and we will move these cases to completion while reducing our operations in Nepal.

We continue to face challenges accessing refugee applicants in a variety of locations. In some countries, such as Syria, Yemen, and Eritrea, Department of Homeland Security (DHS) adjudicators have been unable to travel to interview applicants for several years. DHS-approved refugees in Syria continue to depart as their cases become fully cleared, and we have had applicants in Yemen, Iran, and Eritrea moved to a UNHCR Emergency Transit Center in Romania or Slovakia, but relatively small numbers benefit from this option due to capacity limitations. In Iraq, Lebanon, and Kenya, security concerns have hampered our ability to process applicants. In Chad, Ethiopia, and other countries, applicants are in extremely remote locations, and are hard and expensive to reach. We are constantly reviewing our operations to find efficient and creative ways to access larger numbers of vulnerable individuals in these locations for resettlement.

In these and other ways we will continue to adapt to meet changing needs and keep our refugee resettlement program strong. With the support of Congress and the American people, refugee resettlement will continue to be a proud American tradition for many years to come.

TABLE OF CONTENTS

LIST OF TABLES

Page

I. OVERVIEW OF U.S. REFUGEE POLICY

At the end of 2013, the estimated refugee population worldwide stood at 16.7 million, with 11.7 million under the mandate of the United Nations High Commissioner for Refugees (UNHCR). The United States actively supports efforts to provide protection, assistance, and durable solutions to these refugees, as these measures fulfill our humanitarian interests and further our foreign policy and national security interests. Under the authority of the Migration and Refugee Assistance Act of 1962, as amended, the United States contributes to the programs of UNHCR, the International Committee of the Red Cross (ICRC), the International Organization for Migration (IOM), the United Nations Relief and Works Agency for Palestine Refugees in the Near East (UNRWA), and other international and non-governmental organizations that provide protection and assistance to refugees, internally displaced persons (IDPs), victims of conflict, stateless persons, and other vulnerable migrants. These contributions are used to address the legal and physical protection needs of refugees and to furnish basic assistance such as water, sanitation, food, health care, shelter, education, and other services. The United States monitors these programs to ensure the most effective use of resources, maximizing humanitarian impact for the beneficiaries.

The United States and UNHCR recognize that most refugees desire safe, voluntary return to their homeland. During FY 2014, the United States continued to support voluntary repatriation programs around the world. Refugee repatriation operations brought refugees home to Afghanistan, Cote d'Ivoire, the Democratic Republic of Congo (DRC), and Sri Lanka. These operations were carried out to protect returning refugees as well as to help them contribute to the stabilization, reconstruction, and development of their home countries.

Where opportunities for return remain elusive, the United States and partners pursue self-sufficiency and temporary, indefinite, or permanent local integration in countries of asylum. The Department of State encourages host governments to protect refugees and allow them to integrate into local communities. The State Department further promotes local integration by funding programs to enhance refugee self-sufficiency and support community-based social services. Groups that may avail themselves of opportunities for local integration include Afghans in India, Angolans in Zambia, Burundians in Tanzania, Eritreans in Sudan, Liberians and Sierra Leoneans in seven countries across West Africa, and Colombians in Ecuador, Costa Rica, Panama and Venezuela.

UNHCR estimates that there are 10 million people worldwide who are not recognized nationals of any state and are, therefore, legally or de facto stateless. Without recognized citizenship in any country, many stateless persons exist in refugee-like situations, unable to claim rights and denied even the most basic protections of law. The United States has supported UNHCR's efforts to prevent and reduce statelessness, including addressing gaps in citizenship laws, eliminating provisions that discriminate against women, and promoting fair application of those laws. U.S. contributions to UNHCR's core budget support efforts to prevent and address statelessness in Burma, the Dominican Republic, Cote d'Ivoire, Nepal, Sudan, Turkmenistan, and elsewhere. In addition, the Department of State seeks to use the U.S. Refugee Admissions Program (USRAP) to demonstrate leadership and encourage other countries to do more to help stateless people and refugees stuck in protracted situations. This approach is reflected in the current resettlement of Rohingya refugees, as well as in past resettlement of Meskhetian Turks.

The United States and UNHCR recognize that resettlement in third countries is a vital tool for providing refugees protection and/or durable solutions in some particularly difficult cases. For some refugees, resettlement is the best, and perhaps the only, alternative. Stateless refugees who arrive in the United States for resettlement not only find a durable solution to their displacement, but are also placed on a path that will afford the opportunity to naturalize and resolve their stateless status.

For more than a decade, the U.S. government has provided financial support to expand and improve UNHCR's resettlement capacity, principally by providing staff and constructing facilities. As a result, UNHCR has substantially increased referrals to the United States and other resettlement countries. We plan to continue to work with UNHCR and consult with host governments on group referrals. We will continue to assess resettlement needs and allow qualified NGOs to refer refugee applicants to the program.

The United States has also supported UNHCR's efforts to expand the number of countries active in resettlement. In 2013, UNHCR referred refugees to 27 countries for resettlement consideration. Over 90 percent were referred to the United States, Australia, and Canada. Smaller numbers of referrals were made to Argentina, Brazil, Chile, Czech Republic, Denmark, Estonia, Finland, France, Germany, Hungary, Iceland, Ireland, Italy, Netherlands, New Zealand, Norway, Portugal, Republic of Korea, Slovakia, Spain, Sweden, Switzerland, Uruguay, and the United Kingdom.

While the overall number of refugees referred by UNHCR and the percentage resettled by various countries fluctuate from year to year, the United States aims to ensure at least 50 percent of all refugees referred by UNHCR worldwide are considered for resettlement in the United States, depending on the availability of funds. Some 67 percent of UNHCR-referred refugees who were resettled in 2013, were resettled in the United States (see Table VIII).

The foreign policy and humanitarian interests of the United States are often advanced by addressing refugee issues in first asylum and resettlement countries. In some cases, the United States has been able to use its leadership position in resettlement to promote and secure other durable solutions for refugees, or advance other human rights or foreign policy objectives. The United States is by far the largest single donor to UNHCR, providing over $1.05 billion in FY 2013. During the past few years, U.S. resettlement efforts in Africa, the Middle East, and East Asia have helped energize efforts by UNHCR and other countries to ensure that first asylum is maintained for larger refugee populations or that local integration or third country resettlement are options offered to those in need. In certain locations, the prompt resettlement of politically sensitive cases has helped defuse regional tensions.

During its history, the USRAP has responded to changing circumstances. The end of the Cold War dramatically altered the context in which the USRAP operated. The program shifted its focus away from large groups concentrated in a few locations (primarily refugees from Vietnam, the former Soviet Union, and the former Yugoslavia) and began to admit refugees representing over 50 nationalities per year. Interviews of refugees by American officials from the Department of Homeland Security's U.S. Citizenship and Immigration Services (USCIS) are often conducted in remote locations and are geared toward populations in greatest need of third country resettlement opportunities.

While maintaining the United States' leadership role in humanitarian protection, an integral part of this mission is to ensure that refugee resettlement opportunities go to those who are eligible for such protection and do not present a risk to the safety and security of our country. Accordingly, the USRAP is committed to deterring and detecting fraud among those seeking to resettle in the United States and continues to employ the most rigorous security measures possible to protect against threats to our national security.

Refugees resettled in the United States enrich our nation. The USRAP is premised on the idea that refugees should become economically self-sufficient as quickly as possible. The Department of State works domestically with agencies participating in the Reception and Placement (R&P) program to ensure that refugees receive services in the first thirty to ninety days after arrival in accordance with established standards. During and after the initial resettlement period, the Office of Refugee Resettlement at the Department of Health and Human Services (HHS/ORR) provides leadership, technical assistance, and funding to states, the District of Columbia, and nonprofit organizations to help refugees become self-sufficient and integrated into U.S. society. ORR programs use formula and discretionary grants to provide cash and medical assistance, employment and training programs, and other services to newly arriving and recently arrived refugees. Moreover, upon arrival, refugees are Americans in waiting. Refugees are immediately eligible for lawful employment and after one year, are required to apply for adjustment of status to lawful permanent resident. Five years after admission, a refugee who has been granted lawful permanent resident status is eligible to apply for citizenship.

A number of factors create challenges for resettlement agencies striving to meet the needs of refugees in the program. The refugee population is ever more linguistically diverse, with wide-ranging educational and employment histories. To better prepare refugees for arrival in the United States, the USRAP continues to improve overseas cultural orientation, including thorough curricula review and teacher training. In 2013, we determined via two pilot rounds of English as a Second Language classes for some refugees in Kenya, Thailand, and Nepal that the classes provided basic English competency and promoted continued language learning after arrival in the United States. As a result, we began to fund our Resettlement Support Center for Africa to provide ESL to some Congolese prior to resettlement in the United States. We intend to continue this funding in 2015.

PROPOSED CEILINGS

TABLE I

REFUGEE ADMISSIONS IN FY 2013 AND FY 2014, PROPOSED REFUGEE ADMISSIONS BY REGION FOR FY 2015[2]

REGION	FY 2013 ACTUAL ARRIVALS	FY 2014 CEILING	FY 2014 PROJECTED ARRIVALS	PROPOSED FY2015 CEILING
Africa	15,980	15,000	15,800	**17,000**
East Asia	16,537	14,000	14,500	**13,000**
Europe and Central Asia	580	1,000	900	**1,000**
Latin America/Caribbean	4,439	5,000	4,300	**4,000**
Near East/South Asia	32,389	33,000	34,000	**33,000**
Regional Subtotal	69,925	68,000	69,500	**68,000**
Unallocated Reserve		2,000		**2,000**
Total	69,925	70,000	69,500	**70,000**

Generally, to be considered a refugee, a person must be outside his or her country of nationality or, if stateless, outside his or her country of last habitual residence. Under the Immigration and Nationality Act (INA) § 101(a)(42)(B), however, the President may specify circumstances under which individuals who are within their countries of nationality or last habitual residence may be considered a refugee for purposes of admission to the United States. The FY 2015 proposal recommends continuing such in-country processing for specified persons in Iraq, Cuba, Eurasia and the Baltics, and commencing such in-country processing for specified persons in Honduras, El Salvador and Guatemala. Persons for whom resettlement is requested by a U.S. ambassador in any location in the world may also be considered, with the understanding that they will only be referred to the USRAP following Department of State consultation with USCIS at the Department of Homeland Security (DHS).

---

[2] These proposed figures assume enactment by Congress of the President's Budget levels related to the U.S. Refugee Admissions Program elements.

Unallocated Reserve

This proposal includes 2,000 unallocated admissions numbers to be used if needed for additional refugee admissions from any region. The unallocated numbers would only be used following notification to Congress.

ADMISSIONS PROCEDURES

Eligibility Criteria

The Department of State's Bureau of Population, Refugees, and Migration (PRM) is responsible for coordinating and managing the USRAP. A critical part of this responsibility is determining which individuals or groups from among the millions of refugees worldwide will have access to U.S. resettlement consideration. PRM coordinates within the Department of State, as well as with DHS/USCIS and other agencies, in carrying out this responsibility.

Section 207(a)(3) of the INA states that the USRAP shall allocate admissions among refugees "of special humanitarian concern to the United States in accordance with a determination made by the President after appropriate consultation." Which individuals are "of special humanitarian concern" to the United States for the purpose of refugee resettlement consideration is determined through the USRAP priority system. There are currently three priorities or categories of cases:

- Priority 1 – Individual cases referred to the program by virtue of their circumstances and apparent need for resettlement;
- Priority 2 – Groups of cases designated as having access to the program by virtue of their circumstances and apparent need for resettlement;
- Priority 3 – Individual cases from designated nationalities granted access for purposes of reunification with anchor family members already in the United States.

(Note: Refugees resettled in the United States may also seek the admission of spouses and unmarried children under 21 who are still abroad by filing a "Following to Join" petition, which obviates the need for a separate refugee claim adjudication. This option is described in more detail in the discussion of Following to Join cases below.)

Access to the program under one of the above-listed processing priorities does not mean an applicant meets the statutory definition of "refugee" or is admissible to the United States under the INA. Applicants who are eligible for access within the established priorities are presented to DHS/USCIS officers for interview. The ultimate determination as to whether an applicant can be admitted as a refugee is made by DHS/USCIS in accordance with criteria set forth in the INA and various security protocols.

Although the access categories to the USRAP are referred to as "processing priorities," it is important to note that entering the program under a certain priority does not establish precedence in the order in which cases will be processed. Once cases are established as eligible for access under one of the three processing priorities, they all undergo the same processing steps.

PRIORITY 1 – INDIVIDUAL REFERRALS

Priority 1 (P-1) allows consideration of refugee claims from persons of any nationality[3], usually with compelling protection needs, for whom resettlement appears to be the appropriate durable solution. Priority 1 cases are identified and referred to the program by UNHCR, a U.S. Embassy, or a designated NGO. UNHCR, which has the international mandate worldwide to provide protection to refugees, has historically referred the vast majority of cases under this priority. Some NGOs providing humanitarian assistance in locations where there are large concentrations of refugees have also undergone training by PRM and DHS/USCIS and have been designated eligible to provide Priority 1 referrals.

Process for Priority 1 Individual Referral Applications

Priority 1 referrals from UNHCR and NGOs are generally submitted to the appropriate Regional Refugee Coordinator, who forwards the referrals to the appropriate Resettlement Support Center (RSC) for case processing and scheduling of the DHS/USCIS interview. PRM's Office of Admissions reviews embassy referrals for completeness and may consult with DHS in considering these referrals.

A U.S. ambassador may make a Priority 1 referral for persons still in their country of origin if the ambassador determines that such cases are in need of exceptional treatment and the Departments of State (PRM) and Homeland Security (DHS/USCIS) concur. In some cases, a Department of State request to DHS/USCIS for parole may be a more appropriate option.

---

[3] Referrals of North Koreans and Palestinians require State Department and DHS/USCIS concurrence before they may be granted access to the USRAP.

PRIORITY 2 – GROUP REFERRALS

Priority 2 (P-2) includes specific groups (within certain nationalities, clans or ethnic groups, sometimes in specified locations) identified by the Department of State in consultation with DHS/USCIS, NGOs, UNHCR, and other experts as being in need of resettlement. Some Priority 2 groups are processed in their country of origin. The process of identifying the group and its characteristics includes consideration of whether the group is of special humanitarian concern to the United States and whether members of the group will likely be able to qualify for admission as refugees under U.S. law. Groups may be designated as Priority 2 during the course of the year as circumstances dictate, and the need for resettlement arises. PRM plays the coordinating role for all group referrals to the USRAP.

There are two distinct models of Priority 2 access to the program: open access and predefined group access, normally upon the recommendation of UNHCR. Under both models, Priority 2 designations are made based on shared characteristics that define the group. In general, the possession of these characteristics is the reason the group has been persecuted in the past or faces persecution in the future.

The open-access model for Priority 2 group referrals allows individuals to seek access to the program on the basis of meeting designated criteria. To establish an open-access Priority 2 group, PRM, in consultation with DHS/USCIS, and (as appropriate) with UNHCR and others, defines the specific criteria for access. Once the designation is in place, applicants may approach the program at any of the processing locations specified as available for the group to begin the application process. Applicants must demonstrate that they meet specified criteria to establish eligibility for access.

The open-access model has functioned well in the in-country programs, including the long-standing programs in Eurasia and the Baltics, and in Cuba. It was also used successfully for Vietnamese for nearly thirty years (1980-2009), Bosnian refugees during the 1990s, and is now in use for Iranian religious minorities and Iraqis with links to the United States.

The RSCs responsible for handling open-access Priority 2 applications, working under the direction of PRM, make a preliminary determination as to whether the applicants qualify for access and should be presented to DHS/USCIS for interview. Applicants who clearly do not meet the access requirements are "screened out" prior to DHS/USCIS interview.

In contrast to an open-access group, a predefined group designation is normally based on a UNHCR recommendation that lays out eligibility criteria that should apply to individuals in a specific location. Once PRM, in consultation with DHS/USCIS has established the access eligibility criteria for the group, the referring entity (usually UNHCR) provides the bio data of eligible refugee applicants for processing. This type of group referral is advantageous in situations in which the intensive labor required to generate individual referrals would be impracticable, potentially harmful to applicants due to delays, or counterproductive. Often, predefined groups are composed of persons with similar persecution claims. The predefined group referral process saves steps and can conserve scarce resources, particularly for UNHCR. In recent years, predefined groups have included certain Burmese in Thailand, certain Bhutanese in Nepal, and certain Congolese in Rwanda. Predefined group referrals with clear, well-defined eligibility criteria and several methods for cross-checking group membership can serve as a fraud deterrent as well, preventing non-group members from gaining access to the USRAP by falsely claiming group membership. It can also speed the resettlement process in cases where immediate protection concerns are present.

FY 2015 Priority 2 Designations

In-country processing programs

The following ongoing programs that process individuals still in their country of origin under Priority 2 group designations will continue in FY 2015:

Eurasia and the Baltics
This Priority 2 designation applies to Jews, Evangelical Christians, and Ukrainian Catholic and Orthodox religious adherents identified in the Lautenberg Amendment, Public Law No. 101-167, § 599D, 103 Stat. 1261 (1989) (codified at 8 U.S.C. § 1157) as amended ("Lautenberg Amendment"), with close family in the United States. With annual renewal of the Lautenberg Amendment, these individuals are considered under a reduced evidentiary standard for establishing a well-founded fear of persecution.

Cuba
Included in this Priority 2 program are human rights activists, members of persecuted religious minorities, former political prisoners, forced-labor conscripts, and persons deprived of their professional credentials or subjected to other disproportionately harsh or discriminatory treatment resulting from their perceived or actual political or religious beliefs.

Iraqis Associated with the United States

Under various Priority 2 designations, including those set forth in the Refugee Crisis in Iraq Act, employees of the U.S. Government, a U.S. government-funded contractor or grantee, U.S. media or U.S. NGOs working in Iraq, and certain family members of such employees, as well as beneficiaries of approved I-130 (immigrant visa) petitions, are eligible for refugee processing in Iraq.

The following planned program that would process individuals still in their country of origin under a Priority 2 group designation may be launched in FY 2015:

Minors in Honduras, El Salvador, and Guatemala

Under this planned new P-2 program, certain lawfully present qualifying relatives in the United States could request access to a refugee interview for an unmarried child under 21 in his/her country of origin.

Groups of Humanitarian Concern outside the Country of Origin

The following Priority 2 groups are already designated and, in most cases, undergoing processing with significant arrivals anticipated during FY 2014. (Additional Priority 2 groups may be designated over the course of the year.)

Ethnic Minorities and others from Burma in camps in Thailand

Under this existing Priority 2 designation, individuals who have fled Burma, are registered in nine refugee camps along the Thai/Burma border, are identified by UNHCR as in need of resettlement, and expressed interest prior to January 2014 (depending on the location), are eligible for processing.

Ethnic Minorities from Burma in Malaysia

Under this Priority 2 designation, ethnic minorities from Burma who are recognized by UNHCR as refugees in Malaysia and identified as being in need of resettlement are eligible for processing.

Bhutanese in Nepal

Under this existing Priority 2 designation, Bhutanese refugees registered by UNHCR in camps in Nepal, identified as in need of resettlement, and expressed interest prior to June 30, 2014, are eligible for processing.

Iranian Religious Minorities
Under this Priority 2 designation, Iranian members of certain religious minorities are eligible for processing and are considered under a reduced evidentiary standard for establishing a well-founded fear of persecution, pursuant to annual renewal of the Lautenberg Amendment as amended in 2004 by Sec. 213 of Title II, Division E, of the Consolidated Appropriations Act of 2004, P.L. 108-199, 118 Stat. 3 ("the Specter Amendment").

Iraqis Associated with the United States
Under various Priority 2 designations, including those set forth in the Refugee Crisis in Iraq Act, employees of the U.S. government, a U.S. government-funded contractor or grantee, U.S. media or U.S. NGOs working in Iraq, and certain family members of such employees, as well as beneficiaries of approved I-130 (immigrant visa) petitions, are eligible for refugee processing. This program is operating in Jordan and Egypt, in addition to the in-country program in Iraq.

Congolese in Rwanda
Under this existing Priority 2 designation, certain Congolese refugees in Rwanda who were verifiably registered in 1997 and identified as in need of resettlement are eligible for processing.

PRIORITY 3 – FAMILY REUNIFICATION

The Priority 3 (P-3) category affords USRAP access to members of designated nationalities who have immediate family members in the United States who initially entered as refugees or were granted asylum. At the beginning of each fiscal year, PRM, in consultation with DHS/USCIS, establishes the list of nationalities eligible for processing under this priority. The PRM Assistant Secretary may modify the list during the year, in consultation with DHS/USCIS, but additions or deletions are generally made to coincide with the fiscal year.

Inclusion on the P-3 list represents a finding by PRM that the nationality is of special humanitarian concern to the United States for the purpose of family-reunification refugee processing. Eligible nationalities are selected following careful review of several factors. UNHCR's annual assessment of refugees in need of resettlement, provides insight into ongoing refugee situations, which could create the need for family-reunification processing. In addition, prospective or ongoing repatriation efforts and U.S. foreign policy interests must be weighed in determining which nationalities should be eligible.

The P-3 program has undergone significant changes in recent years. In order to qualify for access under the P-3 program, an applicant must be outside of his or her country of origin, be registered or have legal status in the country of asylum (with some exceptions), have had an Affidavit of Relationship (AOR) filed on his or her behalf by an eligible "anchor" relative in the United States during a period in which the nationality was included on the eligibility list, and have been cleared for onward processing by the DHS/USCIS Refugee Access Verification Unit (RAVU).

Since the P-3 program resumed in October 15, 2012, after a suspension period due to fraud concerns, the AOR has been an official Department of State form (DS-7656). The form contains new language about penalties for committing fraud, and alerts filers that DNA evidence of certain claimed biological parent-child relationships will be required in order to gain access to a USCIS interview for refugee admission to the United States through the P-3 program. As of June 30, we have received more than 2,000 AORs that are in various stages of processing. We anticipate that P-3 arrivals to the United States will begin in FY2015.

The following family members of the U.S.-based anchor are qualified for P-3 access: spouses, unmarried children under 21, and/or parents. Qualifying anchors are persons who were admitted to the United States as refugees or were granted asylum, including persons who are lawful permanent residents or U.S. citizens who initially were admitted to the United States as refugees or were granted asylum. The anchor relative must be at least 18 years of age at the time the AOR is filed and must file the AOR within 5 years of the date the anchor entered the U.S. as a refugee or was granted asylum.

In addition to the qualifying family members of a U.S.-based anchor listed above, the qualifying family member's spouse and unmarried children under 21 may derive refugee status from the principal applicant for refugee status. On a case-by-case basis, an individual may be added to a qualifying family member's P-3 case if that individual:

1) lived in the same household as the qualifying family member in the country of nationality or, if stateless, last habitual residence; AND
2) was part of the same economic unit as the qualifying family member in the country of nationality or, if stateless, last habitual residence; AND
3) demonstrates exceptional and compelling humanitarian circumstances that justify inclusion on the qualifying family member's case.

These individuals "are not "spouses" or "children", under INA 207(c)(2)(A)" and thus cannot derive their refugee status from the Principal Applicant. They must, therefore, independently establish that they qualify as a refugee.

FY 2015 Priority 3 Nationalities

P-3 processing is available to individuals of the following nationalities:

Afghanistan
Bhutan
Burma
Burundi
Central African Republic
Colombia
Cuba
Democratic People's Republic of Korea (DPRK)
Democratic Republic of Congo (DRC)
El Salvador
Eritrea
Ethiopia
Guatemala
Haiti
Honduras
Iran
Iraq
Mali
Somalia
South Sudan
Sri Lanka
Sudan
Syria
Uzbekistan

FOLLOWING-TO-JOIN FAMILY REUNIFICATION PETITIONS

Under 8 CFR Section 207.7, a principal refugee admitted to the United States may request following-to-join benefits for his or her spouse and/or unmarried children under the age of 21 who were not previously granted refugee status. Once in the United States, and within two years of admission, the refugee may file a Form I-730 Refugee/Asylee Relative Petition[4] with DHS/USCIS for each eligible family member. If the Form I-730 petition is approved by DHS/USCIS (signifying adequate proof of eligibility based on a file review), the National Visa Center then forwards the petition to the embassy or consulate nearest to the location of the beneficiary for travel eligibility.

Cases gaining access to the USRAP through an approved I-730 petition are interviewed by DHS/USCIS or consular officers to verify the relationships claimed in the petition, as well as to examine any applicable bars to status and admissibility to the United States. The beneficiaries are not required to demonstrate persecution claims, as they derive their status from the refugee relative in the United States who filed the petition. Beneficiaries of I-730 petitions may be processed within their country of origin or in other locations.

Anchor relatives in the United States may file an I-730 Refugee/Asylee Relative Petition and seek Priority 3 access (if eligible) simultaneously. In some cases, the I-730 petition will be the only option as the family members are still in their country of origin. It is also important to note that the I-730 or "follow-to-join" process does not allow the relative in the United States to petition for parents as the P-3 process does.

DHS/USCIS REFUGEE ADJUDICATIONS

Section 207(c) of the INA grants the Secretary of the Department of Homeland Security authority to admit, at his/her discretion, any refugee who is not firmly resettled in a third country, who is determined to be of special humanitarian concern, and who is admissible to the United States. The authority to determine eligibility for refugee status has been delegated to USCIS. Beginning in FY 2006, DHS/USCIS restructured the Refugee Affairs Division and established the Refugee Corps, a specially trained cadre of officers dedicated to adjudicating applications for refugee status. The Refugee Corps provides DHS/USCIS with the necessary resources and flexibility to respond to an increasingly diversified refugee admissions program. Each quarter of the fiscal year, on average, USCIS deploys approximately 100 Refugee Officers, Supervisory Refugee Officers, and fingerprinters to 12-16 locations around the world to interview refugee applicants. DHS/USCIS has also substantially enhanced its security vetting, anti-fraud, and training capacity related to refugee processing.

---

[4] This petition is used to file for the relatives of both refugees and asylees, also known as Visa 93 and Visa 92 cases respectively. The Refugee Admissions Program handles only Visa 93 cases, which are counted within the annual refugee admissions ceiling. Visa 92 cases are not considered to be refugee admissions cases and are not counted in the number of refugees admitted annually.

The Eligibility Determination

In order to be approved as a refugee, an applicant must meet the refugee definition contained in § 101(a)(42) of the INA. That section provides that a refugee is a person who is outside his or her country of nationality or last habitual residence and is unable or unwilling to return to that country because of persecution or a well-founded fear of persecution on account of race, religion, nationality, membership in a particular social group, or political opinion. As mentioned above, the President may specify special circumstances under which a person can meet the refugee definition when he or she is still within the country of origin. The definition excludes a person who has ordered, incited, assisted, or otherwise participated in persecution on account of race, religion, nationality, membership in a particular social group, or political opinion. Further, an applicant who has been "firmly resettled" in a third country may not be admitted as a refugee under INA Section207. Applicants are also subject to various statutory grounds of inadmissibility, including criminal, security, and public health grounds, some of which may be waived or from which applicants may be exempted.

The grounds of inadmissibility that apply to refugee applicants include the broad terrorism-related inadmissibility grounds (TRIG) at Section 212(a)(3)(B) of the INA. Beginning in 2005, the Departments of Homeland Security, State, and Justice began to exercise a discretionary Secretarial authority to exempt certain categories of refugee applicants from TRIG inadmissibility based on a determination that they did not represent a threat to the United States and otherwise merited an exemption for humanitarian purposes. As of June 2014, more than 12,700 TRIG exemptions have been granted to refugee applicants.[5]

A DHS/USCIS officer conducts a non-adversarial, face-to-face interview of each refugee applicant designed to elicit information about the applicant's claim for refugee status and any grounds of ineligibility. The officer asks questions about the applicant's experiences in the country of origin, including problems and fears about returning (or remaining), as well as questions concerning the applicant's activities, background, and criminal history. The officer also considers evidence about conditions in the country of origin and assesses the applicant's credibility and claim.

Background Checks

---

[5] Over 6,600 of these exemptions pertained to Burmese applicants who had associations with groups that met the statutory definition of an undesignated "terrorist organization" in Section 212(a)(3)(B). Approximately5,580 of the exemptions related to applicants who provided material support to a terrorist organization under duress – for example, Iraqi applicants who paid a ransom for a kidnapped family member.

Refugee applicants of all nationalities are required to undergo background security checks. Security checks include biographic name checks for all refugee applicants and biometric (fingerprint) checks for refugee applicants aged 14 to 79. PRM, through its overseas Resettlement Support Centers, initiates required biographic name checks, while USCIS is responsible for collecting biometric data for screening. Biographic and biometric information is vetted against a broad array of law enforcement, intelligence community, and other relevant databases to help confirm identity, to check for any criminal or other derogatory information (including watchlist information), and to identify information that could inform lines of questioning during the interview. Refugee applicants must clear all required security checks prior to final approval of their application.

In late 2010, the USRAP implemented an enhanced security check requirement for all refugee applicants. While implementing the enhanced check was critical to strengthening the integrity of the program, refugee admissions were disrupted in FY 2011 and FY 2012. Interagency coordination and processing procedures were improved, however, resulting in increased refugee admissions levels beginning in May 2012. Admissions levels continued at these higher levels in FY 2013 and reached 99.9% of the ceiling set by Presidential Determination.

PROCESSING ACTIVITIES OF THE DEPARTMENT OF STATE

Overseas Processing Services

In most processing locations, PRM engages an NGO, an international organization (IO), or U.S. embassy contractors to manage a Resettlement Support Center (RSC) that assists in the processing of refugees for admission to the United States. RSC staff pre-screen applicants to determine preliminarily if they qualify for one of the applicable processing priorities and to prepare cases for DHS/USCIS adjudication. The RSCs assist applicants in completing documentary requirements and schedule DHS/USCIS refugee eligibility interviews. If an applicant is conditionally approved for resettlement, RSC staff guide the refugee through post-adjudication steps, including obtaining medical screening exams and attending cultural orientation programs. The RSC obtains sponsorship assurances and, once all required steps are completed, refers the case to IOM for transportation to the United States.

In FY 2014, NGOs (Church World Service, Hebrew Immigrant Aid Society, and International Rescue Committee) worked under cooperative agreements with PRM as RSCs at locations in Austria (covering Austria only), Kenya (covering sub-Saharan Africa), and Thailand (covering East Asia). International organizations and NGOs (IOM and the International Catholic Migration Commission) support refugee processing activities based in Ecuador, Jordan, Russia, Nepal, and Turkey covering Latin America, the Middle East, South and Central Asia, and Europe. The U.S. Department of State supports refugee processing in Havana, Cuba.

Cultural Orientation

The Department of State strives to ensure that refugees who are accepted for admission to the United States are prepared for the profound life changes they will experience by providing cultural orientation programs prior to departure for the United States. It is critical that refugees arrive with a realistic idea of what their new lives will be like, what services will be available to them, and what their responsibilities will be.

Every refugee family receives *Welcome to the United States*, a resettlement guidebook developed with contributions from refugee resettlement workers, resettled refugees, and government officials. The 2012 edition is available in eight languages: Arabic, Burmese, Chin, English, Karen, Kinyarwanda, Nepali, and Somali. The previous (2007) edition is still available in 16 languages: Albanian, Amharic, Arabic, Bosnian/Croatian/Serbian, English, Farsi, French, Karen, Kirundi, Nepali, Russian, Somali, Spanish, Swahili, Tigrinya, and Vietnamese. Through this book, refugees have access to accurate information about the initial resettlement period before they arrive. The *Welcome to the United States* refugee orientation video was also revised in 2012 and is available in eight languages: Arabic, Burmese, Chin, English, Karen, Kinyarwanda, Nepali, and Somali. The 2004 version of the video is available in 13 languages: Arabic, English, Farsi, Hmong, Karen, Karenni, Kirundi, Nepali, Russian, Somali, Spanish, Swahili, and Tigrinya.

In addition, the Department of State funds one- to five-day pre-departure orientation classes for eligible refugees at sites throughout the world. In an effort to further bridge the information gap for certain groups, brief video presentations featuring the experience of recently resettled refugees of the same ethnic group are made available to refugee applicants overseas. Groups featured include refugees from Bhutan, Burma, Cuba, Darfur, and Iraq. *Faces of Resettlement*, a video produced in 2013, shows five individuals who entered the United States as refugees, from Bhutan, Burma, Burundi, Iraq, and Sudan. Each of them tells their own story of the ways in which they are rebuilding their lives in their new communities. *Faces of Resettlement* also includes interviews with receiving community members.

Transportation

The Department of State funds the international transportation of refugees resettled in the United States through a program administered by IOM. The cost of transportation is provided to refugees in the form of a loan. Refugees are responsible for repaying these loans over time, beginning six months after their arrival, although it is possible to request a deferral based on inability to begin paying at six months.

Reception and Placement (R&P)

In FY 2014, PRM funded cooperative agreements with nine private resettlement agencies to provide initial resettlement services to refugees arriving in the United States. The R&P agencies are responsible for providing initial reception and core services (including housing, furnishings, clothing and food, as well as assistance with access to medical, employment, educational, and social services) to arriving refugees. These services are provided according to standards of care within a framework of outcomes and indicators developed jointly by the NGO community, state refugee coordinators, and U.S. government agencies. The nine organizations maintain a nationwide network of some 350 affiliated offices in 185 cities to provide services. Two of the organizations also maintain a network of 24 affiliated offices through which unaccompanied refugee minors are placed into foster care, a program administered and funded by HHS/ORR.

Using R&P funds from PRM supplemented by cash and in-kind contributions from private and other sources, the participating agencies provide the following services, consistent with the terms of the R&P cooperative agreement:

- Sponsorship;
- Pre-arrival resettlement planning, including placement;
- Reception on arrival;
- Basic needs support (including housing, furnishings, food, and clothing) for at least 30 days;
- Cultural orientation;
- Assistance with access to health, employment, education, and other services as needed; and
- Development and implementation of an initial resettlement plan for each refugee.

OFFICE OF REFUGEE RESETTLEMENT (ORR)

Through the Refugee Act, Congress directed HHS/ORR to provide refugees with resettlement assistance that includes employment training, English language training, cash assistance (in a manner that promotes early independence), and job placement – including providing women with equal opportunities to employment as men. . ORR's mission is to help refugees transition into the U.S. by providing benefits and assistance that assist them to achieve self-sufficiency and become integrated members of society as soon as possible. To this end, ORR funds and administers various programs, some of which are highlighted below.

State-Administered and Wilson-Fish Programs

Under ORR's state-administered or Wilson-Fish (WF) programs, refugees not eligible for Temporary Assistance for Needy Familes (TANF) or Supplemental Security Income (SSI) are eligible to receive up to eight months of *Refugee Cash Assistance (RCA)*. Refugees not eligible for Medicaid are eligible to receive up to eight months of *Refugee Medical Assistance (RMA)* upon arrival. In state-administered programs that operate a publicly administered RCA program (33 States), RCA benefits are based oncash benefit levels established by state TANF programs. In States that operate their RCA program through a Public-Private Program (PPP) model (5 States) and WF States (12 States plus one county), the RCA benefit is based on the higher of the RCA rates outlined in the ORR regulations or the State TANF rates.

The WF program is an alternative to the traditional state-administered program, and is usually administered by local voluntary resettlement agencies. The WF program emphasizes early employment and economic self-sufficiency by integrating cash assistance, case management, and employment services, and by incorporating innovative strategies for the provision of cash assistance (e.g. financial bonuses for early employment). WF programs also serve as a replacement for the State when the State government withdraws from all or part of the ORR- funded refugee assistance program. There are currently 13 WF programs nationwide.

ORR also provides states/WF programs with *Formula Refugee Social Services (RSS)* and *Targeted Assistance (TAG)* funds. ORR distributes these funds based on arrival numbers and refugee concentration levels in counties with a high utilization of public assistance. Funding is time limited, and refugees can only access RSS and TAG services up to five years after arrival. These services include: employability services, employment assessment services, on-the-job training, English language instruction, vocational training, case management, translation/interpreter services, social adjustment services, health-related services, home management, and if necessary for employment, day care and transportation.

Additionally, to assist specific groups of refugees, ORR administers the following specialized programs through states/WF programs, including Cuban-Haitian, Older Refugees, Preventive Health, Refugee School Impact, and Targeted Assistance.

ORR Matching Grant Program

The ORR Matching Grant program (MG) is provided through the nine national resettlement agencies that provide R & P services and their resettlement affiliates in 42 states. The objective of MG is to guide newly-arrived refugee households toward economic self-sufficiency through employment within four to six months of program eligibility (usually within the first month of arrival). In MG, self-sufficiency is defined as total household income from employment that enables a family unit to support itself without receipt of public cash assistance. ORR awards $2,200 on a per capita basis to each national resettlement agency, which then allocates funds to its local service providers based on projected enrollments. Agencies provide a 50% match to every federal dollar.

Through the ORR Matching Grant Program, local service providers ensure core maintenance services for a minimum of 120 days which include housing, transportation, food, and a cash allowance. Clients also receive intensive case management and employment services. Refugees who are unable to attain self-sufficiency by day 120 or 180, may access RCA for the remainder of the eight month eligibility period. In FY 13, over 29,000 individuals were enrolled in the program, 69% of whom achieved self-sufficiency. Approximately 33% of refugees participate in the ORR Matching Grant Program.

ORR Refugee Health

ORR recently created a Division of Refugee Health (DRH) to address the health and well-being of refugees. DRH is working on various initiatives including: collaborating with partners in the implementation of the Affordable Care Act (ACA), including the expansion of Medicaid and implementation of the state/federal Health Insurance Marketplaces; administering the Survivors of Torture program; providing technical assistance on medical screening guidelines, mental health awareness and linkages, suicide prevention, emergency preparedness and other health and mental health initiatives (e.g. vision care, autism, etc.).

ORR Unaccompanied Refugee Minor (URM) Program

ORR provides funds to 15 states who administer over 20 URM programs. States contract with local licensed foster care agencies that provide specialized placements and services to URMs. URMs live in various placements including: traditional and therapeutic foster homes, group homes, semi-independent and independent living and residential treatment centers, and homes of relatives. URMs receive various services including: English language training, educational and vocational training, cultural preservation, social integration, family tracing, permanency planning, independent living, and health/mental health care. ORR regulations require states to provide services to URM in parity with the state's Title IV-B foster care plan.

Other ORR Discretionary Refugee Service Programs

ORR also provides funding to non-profit agencies to focus on special initiatives or programs for refugees including: case management, ethnic community development, home-based child care business development, individual development accounts, microenterprise development, and agricultural projects.

ORR Technical Assistance

ORR provides technical assistance (TA) to resettlement stakeholders through various organizations that have expertise in certain fields. Currently ORR's TA providers assist stakeholders in the areas of community engagement/integration, employment, health, survivors of torture, and TANFstate programs.

TABLE II

PROPOSED FY 2015 REGIONAL CEILINGS BY PRIORITY

AFRICA

Priority 1 Individual Referrals	14,000
Priority 2 Groups	2,500
Priority 3 Family Reunification Refugees	500
Total Proposed:	**17,000**

EAST ASIA

Priority 1 Individual Referrals	1,800
Priority 2 Groups	11,000
Priority 3 Family Reunification Refugees	200
Total Proposed:	**13,000**

EUROPE / CENTRAL ASIA

Priority 1 Individual Referrals	
Priority 2 Groups	1,000
Priority 3 Family Reunification Refugees	
Total Proposed:	**1,000**

LATIN AMERICA / CARIBBEAN

Priority 1 Individual Referrals	700
Priority 2 Groups	3,250
Priority 3 Family Reunification Refugees	50
Total Proposed:	**4,000**

NEAR EAST / SOUTH ASIA

Priority 1 Individual Referrals	18,450
Priority 2 Groups	14,500
Priority 3 Family Reunification Refugees	50
Total Proposed:	**33,000**

UNALLOCATED RESERVE	**2,000**
TOTAL PROPOSED CEILING:	**70,000**

AFRICA

There are currently some 3.6 million refugees across the African continent, constituting roughly 20 percent of the global refugee population. UN-organized repatriations were still underway in 2014 for refugees able to return to safe areas in northwestern Democratic Republic of Congo (DRC) and Côte d'Ivoire. Organized repatriations to Angola, Burundi, Liberia, and Rwanda have largely been completed, but residual populations remain. UNHCR recommended cessation of prima facie refugee status for refugees from Angola and Liberia effective June 30, 2012, and for pre-1999 caseload Rwandan refugees effective June 30, 2013. Efforts continue to repatriate those who still wish to return and to locally integrate residual populations where asylum countries agree to provide permanent residence or citizenship.

While there has been significant voluntary repatriation among African refugee populations over the past decade, intensified conflict in the Central African Republic, South Sudan, and Nigeria since December 2013 has resulted in some 500,000 new refugees in 2014 to date. In the Central African Republic, violence perpetrated by the predominantly Muslim ex-Séléka forces and the predominantly Christian anti-Balaka militia, together with earlier conflict, has now displaced over 600,000 Central Africans internally and forced nearly 350,000 to flee to neighboring Cameroon, Chad, the DRC, and Republic of the Congo. In South Sudan, conflict erupted in December 2013 between political factions and quickly escalated into a major conflict along ethnic lines. Over 900,000 South Sudanese have been internally displaced and refugee numbers have now reached over 430,000. In Nigeria, terrorist attacks by Boko Haram rebels and reprisals by government forces have displaced an estimated 500,000 in northern Nigeria. Nearly 60,000 people have been uprooted in Nigeria, including more than 15,000 refugees to neighboring Niger and Cameroon.

Ongoing conflict in the DRC, Sudan, and Somalia has also continued to generate new refugee outflows over the past year. Intensified conflict in eastern DRC since mid-2012 has led an additional 170,000 Congolese to seek asylum in Uganda, Rwanda, and Burundi. Additionally, the persistent threat of attack posed by the Lord's Resistance Army (LRA) in northeastern DRC as well as southeastern CAR continues to cause instability in the region, preventing the return of some 40,000 refugees and 400,000 IDPs displaced by the LRA since 2008. In Sudan, renewed fighting between the Sudanese government and Darfur rebels resulted in more than 40,000 new Darfuri refugees fleeing to Chad, bringing the total number to more than 350,000. At the same time, the ongoing Sudanese conflict with rebel groups in Southern Kordofan and Blue Nile states has forced some 253,000 Sudanese refugees to flee to South Sudan, Ethiopia, and

Kenya since June 2011. In Somalia, still the largest refugee generating country in Africa with 1 million refugees, small scale conflict and food insecurity continues to generate new refugees from some areas while improved conditions in other parts of the country has led to some spontaneous refugee returns. Some 26,000 Somalis fled to neighboring countries in 2013, while over 34,000 refugees returned to Somalia in the same year, though most on a temporary basis. The steady outflow of Eritreans also continues, not only to refugee camps in Ethiopia and eastern Sudan, but also further north as Eritreans attempt to migrate to Europe and Israel. More than 300,000 Eritreans have fled political repression, forced conscription, and economic collapse over the past decade.

Africa has also not been immune to conflicts in the neighboring Near East region. North Africa has long hosted large numbers of Palestinian refugees. The ongoing crisis in Syria has added more than 150,000 new refugees to the region including 136,000 in Egypt and 17,000 in Libya. No progress was made over the past year in seeking a resolution to the Western Saharan conflict that would enable an estimated 90,000 Sahrawi refugees in Algeria to return home.

Most African countries honor the principle of first asylum and most have allowed refugees to remain – and in many cases to effectively economically and/or socially integrate – until voluntary repatriation is possible. Some countries, such as Egypt, have forcibly returned refugees over the past year. For countries growing weary of hosting large refugee caseloads, we continue to advocate for hospitality and first asylum for refugees. And, for those countries that lack formal mechanisms for asylum, we continue to advocate for the establishment of systems in consultation with UNHCR. Morocco in particular has made progress in this regard.

While most African countries adhere to encampment policies for refugees, many have allowed for de facto integration by providing land for refugee farmers or permitting refugees to open small businesses. Some African countries have gone a step further in agreeing to legal local integration of refugees, including the granting of legal permanent residence, the right to work, or voting rights. Several West African countries, including Côte d'Ivoire, The Gambia, Ghana, Guinea, Liberia, Nigeria, and Sierra Leone have initiated programs legalizing the status of long-staying former Liberian and Sierra Leonean refugee populations interested in remaining in asylum countries. Likewise, Zambia and Namibia have offered permanent residence status to more than 10,000 former Angolan refugees. Tanzania, in 2008, announced a plan to grant citizenship to Burundi refugees who fled their country in 1972. Some 165,000 accepted the offer of "naturalization," but most still lack official documentation of their new citizenship.

Religious Freedom

In Sub-Saharan Africa, people are generally free to practice their chosen religions. Governments regularly provide for and respect freedom of religion, although in some countries, such as Eritrea and Sudan, religious freedom is limited, particularly in the midst of ethnic and other conflicts.

The Government of Eritrea is responsible for severe religious freedom abuses in Africa. In recent years the country has engaged in serious religious repression by harassing, arresting, and detaining members of independent evangelical groups, including Pentecostals and Jehovah's Witnesses (who lost certain rights of citizenship for not participating in the 1993 national referendum). Detainees are held in harsh conditions and some have died in custody. The government has also sought greater control over the four State-approved religious groups: the Eritrean Orthodox Church, the Roman Catholic Church, the Evangelical (Lutheran) Church, and the Islamic community. The government reportedly holds individuals who are jailed for their religious affiliation at various locations. Often detainees are not formally charged, accorded due process, or allowed access to their families. While many are ostensibly jailed for evasion of military conscription, significant numbers were being held solely for their religious beliefs; the current estimate is between 1,200-3,000 individuals detained on religious grounds. At least three Jehovah's Witnesses had been detained for 15 years, reportedly for evading compulsory military service, a term far beyond the maximum legal penalty of two years for refusing to perform national service.

In Sudan, the government continues to place restrictions on Christians in a manner that is inconsistent with its obligation to uphold freedom of religion. Although there is no penalty for converting from another religion to Islam, converting from Islam is punishable by death, as was demonstrated in the recent apostasy case of Ms. Meriam Ishag who was sentenced to death though the sentenced was not enforced and she was subsequently released. Authorities express their strong prejudice against conversion by occasionally subjecting converts to intense scrutiny, ostracism, and intimidation, or by encouraging converts to leave the country.

Both Eritrea and Sudan are currently designated as "Countries of Particular Concern" (CPC) for particularly severe violations of religious freedom by the Department of State under the International Religious Freedom Act of 1998. The USRAP continues to be available through Priority 1 referrals to Sudanese, Eritrean, and other refugees who are victims of religious intolerance. Refugees from Eritrea and Sudan with certain refugee or asylee family members in the United States will have access to the USRAP through Priority 3.

In Somalia the provisional federal constitution provides for freedom of religion, although it enshrines Islam as the state religion and prohibits proselytism for any religion other than Islam. Since its inception in July 2012, the Federal Government of Somalia has made incremental progress to establish institutions and expanding its authority, but its capacity to enforce the provisional constitution remains extremely limited, particularly outside of Mogadishu. There have been reports that non-Muslim individuals experience discrimination, violence, and detention because of their religious beliefs. Refugees from Somalia with certain refugee or asylee family members in the United States also have access to the USRAP through Priority 3.

Voluntary Repatriation

Despite new and protracted refugee situations, voluntary repatriation to improved conditions in the home country remains the most common and desirable durable solution. With the conclusion of various peace agreements and the support of the U.S. government and other donors, UNHCR has made great progress in promoting and supporting refugee repatriation and reintegration in Africa. Over the past 20 years, net refugee numbers in Africa have fallen by nearly half (from more than six million at their height in the 1990s to 3.6 million today) even in the face of new outflows.

In West Africa, out of an estimated 300,000 who fled the 2010-2011 election-related violence in Côte d'Ivoire, over 230,000 have now returned home. UNHCR anticipates assisting with the return of an additional 20,000 Ivoirian refugees in 2014. The final round of UNHCR's Liberian repatriation program was completed at the end of December 2012, with more than 155,000 Liberians benefiting from assisted returns since 2004; in all, more than 700,000 Liberians have returned home either spontaneously or with UNHCR assistance. In Mali, while UNHCR is not yet promoting refugee return to northern Mali, refugees are beginning to return spontaneously to safe regions now under government control. Neighboring states still host some 190,000 Malian refugees, but an estimated 22,500 had returned home by April 2014.

In East Africa, the repatriation to South Sudan that started in 2005 was largely concluded in 2011 with the return of more than 370,000 refugees. However, due to growing instability in South Sudan in 2012 and 2013 and the current widespread conflict, all repatriation has stopped and the focus has instead shifted to emergency response to the 300,000 new refugees. No UNHCR-organized repatriation initiatives are currently anticipated for the Darfur region of Sudan or Somalia, where insecurity continues to prevent safe and dignified return. UNHCR, the Government of Kenya, and the Government of Somalia signed a

Somali refugee repatriation framework in 2013 and are engaged in coordination and regional plans for refugee returns when conditions are appropriate in Somalia, but UNHCR does not deem it safe to encourage return to Somalia at this point. Despite the efforts of some asylum countries, including Israel, to repatriate Eritrean refugees, UNHCR has strongly discouraged returns to Eritrea given ongoing political repression and harsh treatment of returnees.

In Central Africa, most organized repatriation to Burundi ended in 2010 and there have been over 500,000 returns since 2002, including over 53,000 of the 1972-caseload refugees who chose not to accept the Government of Tanzania's offer of naturalization. Repatriation of the last of the 1993-era Burundi refugees in Tanzania was completed with the closure of Mtabila Camp in December 2012. Although the majority of Rwandan refugees returned home in the late 1990's, some 50,000-100,000 remain in exile. With the cessation of prima facie refugee status for pre-1999 Rwandan refugees on June 30, 2013, remaining Rwandans may be required either to repatriate or to seek other means of remaining in asylum countries. Repatriation to relatively stable areas of eastern DRC wound down in 2011 with the conclusion of returns from Zambia and Tanzania to Katanga Province, but renewed hostilities between the GDRC and the M23 rebel group—and increased activity of other armed groups across eastern DRC-- erased most of these gains and North and South Kivu provinces and Katanga remain mostly too insecure for large-scale refugee return. Ethnic violence that erupted in late 2009 in Equateur Province forced some 140,000 Congolese to flee to the Central African Republic and the Republic of Congo. A facilitated repatriation for these Congolese refugees began in May 2012; as of April 2014, more than 112,000 refugees have been repatriated back to northwestern DRC and UNHCR hopes to repatriate an additional 20,000 refugees by June 30, 2014.

Local Integration

In a number of protracted situations, refugees have been able to become self-sufficient, and their camps and settlements have been efficiently integrated both economically and socially into the host communities, even as legal rights lag behind. This integration dynamic has occurred particularly for refugees who fled during the 1960s through the early 1980s to countries that had arable land available, allowing many refugees to move out of camps. Despite such de facto integration, refugees residing among the local population did not necessarily enjoy the rights, entitlements, or economic opportunities available to legal residents. As a result, this piecemeal integration was often an interim, rather than a durable, solution for many African refugees.

More recently, however, a number of African countries have offered more formal integration as a durable solution for residual refugee populations who will not or cannot repatriate. In conjunction with UNHCR, the Governments of Côte d'Ivoire, The Gambia, Ghana, Guinea, Liberia, Nigeria, and Sierra Leone launched a regional local integration program for Liberian and Sierra Leonean refugees in 2007. That program provided refugees opportunities for economic self-reliance; activities to enhance the quality of their social integration; and legal rights and documentation, including access to citizenship in some countries and freedom of movement in all countries under the protocols of the Economic Community of West African States (ECOWAS). The Government of Zambia pledged in 2012 to provide permanent residence status to 10,000 former Angolan refugees -- mainly refugees who arrived before 1986, were born in Zambia, or are married to Zambians -- and has already approved 6,000 who meet eligibility criteria. Namibia as well has agreed to legal local integration of 2,400 former Angolan refugees.

Senegal offered Mauritanian refugees who wished to remain in Senegal the option of becoming Senegalese citizens in 2007, and UNHCR, in partnership with the Senegalese government, launched a campaign in 2012 to provide digitized and biometric identity cards to some 19,000 refugees (of whom 14,000 were Mauritanians) by the end of the year. The card guarantees holders the same rights as Senegalese citizens, including the right to residence in the country and to travel to ECOWAS member states. The Governments of Uganda and Mozambique have previously stated their intention to provide refugees with local integration opportunities and citizenship, but have not yet passed the required legislation. As mentioned above, the Government of Tanzania offered to provide permanent settlement and citizenship to nearly 200,000 1972-era Burundi refugees; some 165,000 accepted the offer and were collectively naturalized, although the vast majority have not yet received documentation and the modalities of the integration process are still being negotiated.

While not formal integration programs, a few countries (Uganda and Niger, for example) have permitted refugees to live or work outside of camps or have temporarily adapted to natural rural to urban migration that involves refugees as well as nationals (for example, Kenya until late 2012). Ethiopia formally introduced an out-of-camp policy for Eritrean refugees in August 2010, allowing Eritreans to live outside camps if they are able to support themselves or if they have someone to sponsor them financially. While it does not give Eritrean refugees the right to work, it does offer additional educational opportunities, including tertiary education. In 2013, Sudan also agreed to issue work permits to some 30,000 Eritrean refugees who wish to work outside of refugee camps in eastern Sudan.

Third-Country Resettlement

Given the political and economic volatility in many parts of Africa, resettlement to third countries outside the region is an essential durable solution and element of protection for certain refugees. With limited opportunities for permanent integration in many countries of asylum and the protracted nature of some refugee situations, the need for third-country resettlement of African refugees is expected to continue. In recent years, UNHCR has increasingly viewed resettlement as an important tool of protection for refugees in Africa and has shown an increase in resettlement referrals this past year.

FY 2014 U.S. Admissions

We project close to 16,000 African refugee arrivals in FY 2014. This number is a result of the increase in processing capacity in a number of countries of asylum.

We expect to admit nearly 12,000 refugees from various processing locations in East and Central Africa. Two countries of origin – Somalia and DRC – account for the vast majority of U.S. refugee admissions from the region, followed by Eritrea, Sudan and Ethiopia. Approximately 4,000 refugees will depart for the United States from Kenya this year, mostly Somalis in Kakuma. Although we have resumed processing in Dadaab intermittently, originally suspended in October 2011, capacity is limited by the security situation and interview slots are generally reserved for the most urgent cases. To reach the remaining refugees pending USCIS adjudication, PRM funded the construction of a transit center in Kakuma camp that can accommodate approximately 2,000 refugees from Dadaab and is currently at capacity. Admissions from Ethiopia continue to be strong with approximately 3,500 U.S. arrivals projected this fiscal year. Populations include Somalis from camps in the east and Eritreans from the northern camps, including approximately 50 Eritrean unaccompanied refugee minors. Implementation of the enhanced Congolese Resettlement Strategy – UNHCR's effort to refer 50,000 DRC refugees for resettlement from Rwanda, Uganda, Tanzania and Burundi to all resettlement countries over the next 5-7 years – continued with increased processing in Rwanda and Uganda. We anticipate strong arrivals from Rwanda and Uganda in FY14, at 2,000 and 1,700 arrivals respectively.

From Southern Africa, we expect to admit 1,300 refugees consisting primarily of Somalis from South Africa and Congolese from Namibia, Zambia, and Zimbabwe. Elsewhere in Africa, we continue to interview refugees from the Central African Republic in southern Chad, Sudanese Darfuri refugees in Eastern Chad and expect to admit nearly 400 refugees altogether from Chad in FY 2014. We restarted resettlement from eastern Chad following a three-year suspension after obtaining the support of the Government of Chad.

Outside of sub-Saharan Africa, we anticipate approximately 2,500 Sudanese, Somali, Ethiopian, Eritrean and other sub-Saharan African refugees who will be arriving primarily from Tunisia, Egypt, Turkey, and Russia or via one of the UNHCR Emergency Transit Centers in Romania and Slovakia. In all, we expect to admit refugees of nearly 30 African nationalities, processed in dozens of countries during FY 2014.

FY 2015 U.S. Resettlement Program

We propose up to 17,000 resettlement numbers for African refugees in FY 2015. PRM has actively engaged relevant offices within the Department of State, UNHCR, the NGO community, and DHS/USCIS to identify caseloads appropriate for resettlement consideration. As a result of these discussions, PRM has identified a number of nationalities and groups for priority processing during FY 2015.

From East Africa, we expect 13,000 admissions. Kenya will continue to be the largest resettlement country departing primarily Somalis. Ethiopia will be the second largest resettlement country with the continued processing of Somalis and Eritreans. We also expect UNHCR to continuing referring Eritrean unaccompanied refugee minors at a rate of about 100 per year from camps in northern Ethiopia. We anticipate that the first successful P-3 family reunification program applicants will arrive in the United States in FY 2015. In the Great Lakes region, processing of Congolese in Rwanda, Uganda, Tanzania, and Burundi will continue, and P-2 processing will continue in Rwanda.

From southern Africa, we expect to admit 1,500 refugees consisting primarily of Somalis from South Africa and Congolese from Mozambique, Malawi, Namibia, Zambia, and Zimbabwe. In Chad, UNHCR intends to rapidly increase the number of referrals in FY 2014 and 2015 to create a robust resettlement program for Sudanese Darfuris in eastern Chad. This will be in addition to the continued processing of Central African Republic refugees from southern Chad.

Outside of sub-Saharan Africa, we anticipate up to 2,000 Sudanese, Somali, Ethiopian, Eritrean and other sub-Saharan African refugees will be admitted from Egypt, Lebanon, Turkey, Jordan, and Russia. Processing in these locations largely depends on the local security situation which will determine if teams of DHS/USCIS refugee officers can access these locations.

Proposed FY 2015 Africa program to include arrivals from the following categories:

Priority 1 Individual Referrals	*14,000*
Priority 2 Groups	*2,500*
Priority 3 Family Reunification	*500*
Total Proposed Ceiling	*17,000*

EAST ASIA

Several East Asian countries host large and diverse refugee populations. Recent years have seen important developments for these groups. Thailand, Malaysia, Bangladesh, and India continue to host large numbers of Burmese refugees and asylum-seekers. The U.S. government continues to press for meaningful political and democratic reform and national reconciliation with ethnic minority groups in Burma, while recognizing reforms made over the past three years by easing sanctions. The international community continues to engage in discussions regarding the voluntary return of Burmese refugees, but acknowledges that ongoing conflict, the pending nationwide ceasefire agreement with armed ethnic groups, peace and national reconciliation efforts, and limited access to provide humanitarian and development assistance make large-scale return of refugees in safety and with dignity a gradual process.

The resettlement of more than 100,000 Burmese refugees from Thailand since 2006 – including more than 75,000 to the United States – has significantly reduced the number of Burmese refugees in the camps who are eligible for the U.S. P-2 resettlement program due to the registration date requirement. After more than seven years of large-scale resettlement, we have arrived at the natural conclusion of the group resettlement program that has specific eligibility criteria for Burmese refugees who were re-registered by UNHCR in 2005 and formally registered by the Royal Thai Government (RTG). Throughout 2013 we conducted rolling announcement deadlines for eligible Burmese refugees to apply for U.S. resettlement that varied by camp based on when resettlement operations began. More than 5,000 eligible Burmese refugees submitted expressions of interest during the announcement period. P-2 processing will continue - with a steady decline in annual departures - until we have completed the processing of every application received by the deadline in each camp. Those who do not exercise this option will be able to remain in the camps until safe and voluntary returns are possible. The United States will continue to accept individual referrals from UNHCR for all nationalities, including Burmese.

Since 2006, UNHCR Malaysia has operated the second largest refugee status determination program in the world and it is currently the largest single country in the U.S. resettlement program with some 9,000 projected refugee departures in FY14 and more than 51,000 since 2006. As of the end of March 2014, there were 143,435 persons of concern registered with UNHCR in Malaysia of which 133,070, or 92.8 percent, are from Burma. In addition, some 10,365 asylum-seekers and refugees from various countries – primarily Afghanistan, Iraq, Somalia, and Sri Lanka – are registered with UNHCR in Malaysia. Malaysia is not a party to the 1951 Convention relating to the Status of Refugees or its 1967 Protocol, but generally tolerates the presence of refugees.

The systematic and continuous persecution of the Rohingya, an ethnic, linguistic, and religious minority from Rakhine State, Burma who are de jure stateless by Burmese law, have resulted in large numbers seeking safety in Bangladesh and in other neighboring countries for over five decades. The most recent large influx of approximately 250,000 Rohingya from Rakhine State to the Cox's Bazar district in southeastern Bangladesh began in July 1991. Since then, small but steady flows of Rohingya continue to arrive, with a spike after hundreds of thousands fled to Bangladesh and neighboring countries following the June and October 2012 violence in Rakhine State. Between 1992 and 2005, over 236,000 UNHCR-registered Rohingya refugees were voluntarily repatriated from Cox's Bazar to Rakhine State, most of them immediately after their arrival. No repatriation operation has taken place since. UNHCR currently supports some 30,000 refugees who remain in two official refugee camps (Kutupalong and Nayapara) in Cox's Bazar. An additional 9,000 unregistered Rohingya reside in an unofficial settlement in Leda and approximately 26,000 unregistered Rohingya reside in the makeshift Kutupalong site, adjacent to the official Kutupalong refugee camp. In addition, the Government of Bangladesh (GOB) estimated that 200,000 – 500,000 undocumented Rohingya are currently residing in various villages and towns outside the refugee camps, while UNHCR estimates approximately 200,000 living in Cox's Bazar, Bandarban, and Chittagong districts. UNHCR continues to work to improve the protection environment, promote greater self-reliance, ensure access to essential services, and continue advocacy for durable solutions for both registered refugees and undocumented Rohingya populations.

The cases of more than 500 individual Rohingya in Bangladesh, including 281 individuals approved for resettlement to several countries, have been on hold since October 2010 when the GOB halted third-country resettlement activities pending a review of their refugee policy. In February 2014, the GOB announced its national strategy on "Myanmar Refugees and Undocumented Myanmar Nationals in Bangladesh." The U.S. government is encouraged by GOB commitments made in the national strategy, particularly to survey and list the undocumented Rohingya and to allow third country resettlement to continue. We are prepared to resume resettlement activity immediately upon notification by the GOB that we may proceed. In addition, we expect ongoing UNHCR referrals of urban Burmese in India.

As reflected in the North Korean Human Rights Act, the United States remains deeply concerned about the human rights situation of North Koreans both inside the Democratic People's Republic of Korea (DPRK) and in various countries in the region. The United States began resettling interested, eligible North Korean refugees and their family members in 2006 and remains committed to continuing this program.

Religious Freedom

Although many governments in East Asia do not restrict religious freedom, religious believers face serious persecution in several countries. The DPRK, China, and Burma are designated by the Department of State as Countries of Particular Concern (CPCs) under the International Religious Freedom Act of 1998 for systematic, ongoing, and egregious violations of religious freedom.

The DPRK severely restricts religious freedom, including organized religious activity, except that which is supervised tightly by officially recognized groups linked to the government. Although the DPRK constitution provides for "freedom of religious belief," genuine religious freedom does not exist. Information about the day-to-day life of religious persons in the country is limited. Religious and human rights groups outside of the country have provided numerous reports that members of underground churches have been beaten, arrested, tortured, or killed because of their religious beliefs.

While the constitutions of China, Burma, and Vietnam provide for freedom of religion, in practice, these governments restrict or repress religious activities of some members of religious communities in a manner that is inconsistent with their commitments to uphold freedom of religion.

The Chinese government continues to harass and interfere with unregistered religious groups, most notably the unofficial Catholic churches loyal to the Holy See, Protestant "house churches," some Muslim groups (especially ethnic Uighur Muslims in the Xinjiang Uighur Autonomous Region), members of the Falun Gong, and Tibetan Buddhists reverent to the Dalai Lama. China additionally reprimanded members of government-sanctioned churches for advocacy on behalf of their church communities. Certain religious or spiritual groups are banned by law. The criminal law defines banned groups as "evil cults" and those belonging to them can be sentenced to prison. This includes Falun Gong and some other qigong-based groups, in addition to some Christian groups. Although legislation officially abolished the Reeducation Through Labor (RTL) system in December 2013, religious believers have been harassed, arrested, detained in "black jails" without due process and sentenced to long jail terms. There have been credible allegations of torture.

In Burma, the government implemented considerable political and economic reforms, resulting in improved respect for many human rights. While some deficiencies in respect for and protection of the right to religious freedom continued, the government continued to support interfaith dialogue and provided some members of the international community and international organizations greater access to ethnic minority areas. However, the government continues to discriminate against religious minorities. Antidiscrimination laws do not apply to ethnic groups not formally recognized under the law as citizens, including the Muslim Rohingya in northern Rakhine State, and some other ethnic groups. Incidents of violence against Rohingya increased beginning in 2012 and have carried over into 2014. Further, societal abuses and discrimination based on a mix of ethnicity and religious affiliation, belief or practice occurred.

Vietnam and the United States signed an agreement on religious freedom in May 2005, under which Vietnam committed to improving the status of religious freedom in Vietnam. As a result of the progress Vietnam made after signing the agreement, the U.S. Government removed Vietnam from the CPC list in November 2006. Over the past three years, Vietnam's religious freedom record has been mixed. Progress has been made with regard to the registration/recognition of religious groups and congregations. In addition, religious groups have experienced expanded freedom of assembly. However, there are also reports of harassment at the local level, including through the use of land laws. Several Protestant congregations in rural areas continue to report harassment, including beatings and forced renunciations.

Nationals of the DPRK, Vietnam, China, Laos, and Burma have access to the U.S. Refugee Admissions Program. North Korean and Burmese refugees also have access to family reunification processing through Priority 3.

Voluntary Repatriation

Although the Burmese government has taken steps to implement significant democratic and political reforms, ongoing fighting continues in Kachin and northern Shan States, and tensions remain high in Rakhine State since the June and October 2012 violence. Since 2011, Burmese President Thein Sein's reform-minded administration has been working towards a national peace process. We are hopeful that substantial progress towards this goal will be made in the near future. Further, the post-ceasefire peace process will require resolution of unresolved political grievances. Therefore, the voluntary repatriation of most Burmese refugees and asylum seekers in Thailand, Bangladesh, Malaysia, India and elsewhere is not a viable solution in the immediate future.

Local Integration

Due to fears of a "pull factor," countries in the region have traditionally been reluctant to integrate refugees or to grant asylum. We hope that U.S. efforts to resettle large numbers of refugees from the camps along the Thailand-Burma border will encourage the RTG to allow greater opportunities for livelihood, vocational training and other skills-building activities for those refugees who will not be resettled. The United States and other donor governments continue to engage regularly with the RTG concerning the future of the nine camps on the Thailand-Burma border. Local integration remains a difficult option, due to opposition from host countries, such as Thailand, Bangladesh, Malaysia, and India. UNHCR and the international community continue to advocate for these governments to make policy changes relating to refugees, and to expand humanitarian protection and assistance space for refugees, asylum seekers and other persons of concern.

Third-Country Resettlement

The United States continues to lead third country resettlement efforts in the region. Other countries, including Australia, Canada, New Zealand, and the Nordic countries, resettle refugees referred by UNHCR. In FY 2014, the United States processed UNHCR-referred refugee cases in China, the Hong Kong Special Administrative Region, Indonesia, Malaysia, and Thailand.

In March 2014, UNHCR informed us that it had identified more than two thousand registered Burmese Chin refugees in Malaysia with duplicate biographical data who may have gained access to the U.S. Refugee Admissions Program using fraudulent identities. The cases of these refugees who had not departed Malaysia were immediately placed on hold pending the results of UNHCR's investigation. UNHCR's preliminary findings suggest that the vast majority of Burmese Chin refugees who committed identity fraud did so in order to register with UNHCR and obtain a registration document as protection from arrest and deportation, and not to obtain resettlement. The Department of Homeland Security is reviewing the cases of Burmese Chin refugees who have arrived in the United States whose duplicate identities have been flagged. Routine processing and departure of refugee cases not involved in the fraud investigation continues.

FY 2014 U.S. Admissions

We expect to admit up to 15,000 refugees from East Asia in FY 2014. This will include close to 5,000 Burmese ethnic minorities (mostly Karen, Karenni, and Kachin) living in camps along the Thai-Burma border, some 9,000 Burmese (of various ethnic minorities) in Malaysia, and a small number of urban refugees of various nationalities in the region.

FY 2015 U.S. Resettlement Program

We expect to admit up to 13,000 refugees from East Asia in FY 2015. This will include up to 3,800 Burmese ethnic minorities (mostly Karen and Karenni) living in camps along the Thai-Burma border, some 7,500 Burmese (of various ethnic minorities) in Malaysia, and a small number of urban refugees of various nationalities in the region.

Proposed FY 2015 East Asia program to include arrivals from the following categories:

Priority 1 Individual Referrals	*1,800*
Priority 2 Groups	*11,000*
Priority 3 Family Reunification	*200*
Total Proposed Ceiling	*13,000*

EUROPE AND CENTRAL ASIA

Europe continues to host large refugee populations, as well as other persons affected by conflict, who, over the last two decades, have been left in situations of protracted displacement – often in dire conditions. In its 2012-2013 Global Appeal, UNHCR reported that there were nearly 4.4 million asylum seekers, refugees, internally displaced persons, stateless individuals, or other persons "of concern" throughout Europe and Central Asia. Many had fled conflicts outside the region, such as in Afghanistan and Syria, but the estimates also include persons claiming persecution within Eurasia, including hundreds of thousands of refugees and IDPs in the Balkans and Caucasus.

With the 2012 accession of Bulgaria, Portugal and the Republic of Moldova to the 1954 and 1961 Statelessness Conventions, and Hungary's decision to lift its reservations to the 1954 Convention, 36 of the 49 States in Europe are now party to the 1954 Convention. Twenty-four are party to the 1961 Convention. The Russian Federation and all countries of Central Asia except Uzbekistan have acceded to the 1951 Convention relating to the Status of Refugees and its 1967 Protocol. However, compliance with these instruments remains problematic. Despite sustained efforts by UNHCR and other stakeholders to build protection capacity and help strengthen asylum systems and protection laws in the region, results have thus far been modest. Many of these countries have been slow or reluctant to recognize and integrate refugees and other at-risk individuals. The protection provided by some governments in the region to refugees, asylum seekers, and other migrants is limited and public intolerance, including attacks against non-Slavic foreigners, is common. There are documented cases of refoulement. UNHCR has been working with many of these governments to establish and/or reform asylum procedures and refugee protection laws.

The 1990's break-up of the Soviet Union also created newly independent states with sizeable populations of stateless individuals due to gaps in nationality laws and inconsistent implementation of those laws. Difficulty in establishing citizenship at the time of succession has also created later problems for children born to an undocumented parent(s). The problem of statelessness remains in the region, although some states, such as Turkmenistan, have taken steps to register stateless individuals and facilitate their acquisition of nationality.

According to UNHCR, as of June 2013, there were approximately 408,000 refugees and IDPs in the Balkans, almost all of whom have been displaced for a decade or longer. An estimated 210,000 persons of this population are displaced from Kosovo, most of whom currently live in Serbia. UNHCR estimates that 97,000 individuals in this group are in need of assistance. Since 2000, the overall level of return to Kosovo from Serbia has been low. There have been over 25,000 voluntary returns of minorities to Kosovo since the conflict ended. Housing, documentation issues, a lack of employment opportunity, and occasional violence directed against ethnic Serbs in Kosovo has limited return prospects.

Since 2010, the countries of the region – with the assistance of the international community – made significant progress toward resolving a large part of the refugee situation in the Balkans. A November 2011 ministerial meeting in Belgrade brought together Ministers of Foreign Affairs from Serbia, Croatia, Bosnia and Herzegovina, and Montenegro to sign a Joint Declaration expressing their collective will to resolve the protracted refugee and displacement situation, and they committed their countries to a Regional Housing Program (RHP) for refugees and IDPs supported by international donors. The RHP was designed to create durable solutions for up to 74,000 of the most vulnerable refugees and IDPs in those countries. While principally affecting housing, the RHP has established the Regional Coordination Forum to discuss other pertinent issues such as pensions, civil documentation, exchange of data and other public information. An international donors' conference in April 2012 succeeded in raising over $340 million (€260 million) to support the RHP over five years. The United States provided $10 million in FY 2012, and U.S. involvement is seen as a critical ingredient to the RHP's success. While 12 projects prepared by the four partner countries were approved by the RHP Assembly of Donors in 2013, the implementation start is expected in the summer of 2014.

Despite important steps taken by governments to assist individuals displaced by the collapse of the Soviet Union and related conflicts, many internally displaced persons (IDPs) and returnees still await housing compensation, restitution, or alternative accommodation provision in the North and South Caucasus. The Nagorno-Karabakh War displaced over 800,000 Azerbaijanis in several waves between 1988 and 1994. Today 600,000 IDPs remain, almost 7 percent of Azerbaijan's population. The vast majority live in temporary shelters, administrative buildings, dormitories and hostels, and the government has done little to support integration or aid its displaced population. Armenia received 350,000 refugees from Azerbaijan, of whom almost 3,000 remain as refugees. A large number emigrated to other countries, and nearly 90,000 were ultimately naturalized. Many refugees and former refugees continue to live in unsuitable collective housing or remote villages with insufficient access to government services. A struggling economy and the recent influx of 11,000 Syrian-Armenians has left the government few resources to address refugee concerns, and the country remains dependent on international humanitarian and development assistance. Finally, Georgia has been affected by large population movements since the 1990s as consequences of the breakup of the Soviet Union and the occupation of two regions, Abkhazia and South Ossetia. Although an estimated 147,000 people have returned to their homes in the Gali district (in the Abkhazia region), secured a durable housing solution elsewhere in Georgia, or remained in their original places of residence near the South Ossetia region, approximately 240,000 remain displaced from the 1993 and 2008 wars.

Religious Freedom

The status of religious freedom varies widely across Europe and Central Asia. Some countries place legal restrictions or prohibitions on the wearing of religious attire in schools or in public, particularly impacting Muslims, Jews, Christians, and Sikhs.

Several countries in the region mandate the registration of religious groups. Nontraditional religious groups are sometimes labeled as "sects" or "cults" by their home governments and may be subject to special scrutiny and limited privileges. Registration typically carries the right to rent or own property, hold religious services, appoint military and prison chaplains, and receive state subsidies. Restitution of religious properties is an issue yet to be fully resolved. Uzbekistan is designated by the Department of State as a CPC under the International Religious Freedom Act of 1998 for systematic, ongoing, and egregious violations of religious freedom.

There is a disturbing increase in anti-Semitism and anti-Muslim sentiment in a number of countries in the region, manifested as physical assaults and verbal harassment; hate speech over the internet; and vandalism of cemeteries, synagogues, mosques, and monuments. In several countries, openly anti-Semitic, nationalistic political parties have gained seats in parliaments, with government officials and elected members of parliaments at times responsible for anti-Semitic statements and acts.

Bans on Kosher/Halal slaughter exist in several European countries, while there are increasing calls for bans or restrictions on circumcision, particularly in the Nordic countries. Both circumcision and Kosher/Halal slaughter are religious practices for Jews and Muslims, as well as some other religious groups.

The Russian government uses its anti-extremism law to justify raids, arrests, and bans on religious literature of peaceful, "non-traditional" minority religious groups, including readers of Muslim theologian Said Nursi, Jehovah's Witnesses, Scientologists, Falun Gong practitioners, and some Protestant groups.

In Turkey, some religious minority communities, including Alevis, face difficulties owning property, registering places of worship, training clergy, and obtaining visas for religious workers. Conscientious objectors through their faith are sometimes arrested and prosecuted for failing to comply with laws mandating military service, as previously witnessed in Armenia, Azerbaijan, Belarus, Turkey, and Turkmenistan.

Voluntary Repatriation

The international community continues to support efforts to create favorable conditions for the return of ethnic minorities to their homes in the Balkans. In June 2006, Serbian, Kosovo, and UN authorities signed the Protocol on Voluntary and Sustainable Return to Kosovo, which sought to improve the conditions for return by focusing on three elements: ensuring the safety of returnees, returning property to the displaced and rebuilding their houses, and creating an overall environment that sustains returns. There is still much work to be done in ensuring that those hoping to return have all the means to do so. PRM supported the return process through a grant to Danish Refugee Council in FY 2013 that promoted sustainable return through shelter repair, income-generation activities including vocational training and the provision of agricultural inputs, as well as community development projects to facilitate inter-ethnic dialogue. International funding continues to facilitate and sustain the return and reintegration of displaced minorities from Kosovo. The Regional Housing program will allow thousands of returns to take place in Serbia, Croatia, Bosnia and Herzegovina, and Montenegro. The program will encourage both voluntary repatriation and local integration as durable solutions.

Local Integration

UNHCR has led efforts to create viable asylum systems and effective legal protections for refugees in the Balkans, the Russian Federation, the South Caucasus and Central Asia. However, ineffective implementation of these laws, combined with the history of national animosities and xenophobia throughout the region, often makes effective local integration difficult for ethnic minority refugees. In Azerbaijan, a majority of refugees lack legal status, despite being recognized by UNHCR and permitted by the government to stay in the country. As such, refugees do not have access to legal employment, making local integration in Azerbaijan extremely difficult. In Russia, difficulties in acquiring citizenship remain for some former Soviet citizens who resided in Russia before 1992 and are, under Russian law, entitled to Russian citizenship. Groups such as the Meskhetian Turks have been unable to obtain Russian citizenship and thus remain de facto stateless. In Russia, UNHCR focuses on quality-assurance measures to strengthen the national asylum system, including access to the asylum system at borders, and to contribute to the Government's plans to bring its reception infrastructure and processes up to full international standards. In Montenegro, the path to citizenship has been particularly slow for those displaced from Kosovo. The Regional Housing Program should provide an easier path to local integration for some of the most vulnerable, including Roma populations, among this group. The Government of Serbia is implementing local integration programs for refugees from Bosnia and Herzegovina and Croatia and the displaced persons from Kosovo.

Third-Country Resettlement

The United States continues to accept refugees from the region, almost exclusively religious minorities from Russia and Eurasia processed under the Lautenberg Amendment. Jewish immigration to Israel from the region continues under the United Israel Appeal Program.

FY 2014 U.S. Admissions

In FY 2014 we estimate fewer than 1,000 admissions from Europe and Central Asia. Religious minorities processed under the Lautenberg Amendment from countries of the former Soviet Union constitute nearly the entire caseload. During FY 2014, applicants were processed in Baku, Bishkek, Chisinau, Kyiv, Valletta, Minsk, Odessa, Tbilisi, Moscow, Timisoara, and Humenne.

FY 2015 U.S. Resettlement Program

The proposed FY 2015 ceiling for refugees from Europe and Central Asia is 1,000 individuals. Priority 2 includes individuals who will be processed under Lautenberg guidelines in the states of the former Soviet Union. Low approval rates for this Priority 2 program and a reduced rate of new applications serve to limit the number of admissions.

Proposed FY 2015 Europe and Central Asia program to include arrivals from the following categories:

Priority 1 Individual Referrals	*0*
Priority 2 Groups	*1,000*
Priority 3 Family Reunification	*0*
Total Proposed Ceiling	*1,000*

LATIN AMERICA AND THE CARIBBEAN

In 2014, the number of refugees, asylum seekers, IDPs, and other people of concern in Latin America and the Caribbean approached six million. The ongoing conflict in Colombia generated the largest numbers of refugees and IDPs in the region, and the second largest world-wide. The Government of Colombia (GOC) reports 5.4 million IDPs as of February 2014. Despite an expanded state presence and improved security in cities and towns throughout Colombia, displacement continues. In 2013 the GOC registered 115,000 newly displaced individuals as a result of confrontations between the GOC and illegal armed groups, including the Revolutionary Armed Forces of Colombia (FARC), the National Liberation Army (ELN), criminal gangs (BACRIM) and criminal narco-trafficking networks. According to UNHCR, it is likely that displacement will continue to grow.

In surrounding countries, including Ecuador, Venezuela, Costa Rica, and Panama, there are over 400,000 Colombian asylum seekers and refugees and the number continues to rise. Ecuador has the highest number of recognized Colombian refugees and asylum seekers in Latin America. The Government of Ecuador (GOE) has recognized around 56,640 and UNHCR reports an additional 115,325 persons of concern. The asylum process in Ecuador is slow and difficult to access; the refugee approval rate is around six percent. In May 2012, the GOE issued Presidential Decree 1182, which limited the amount of time that asylum seekers have to file a claim to 15 days. This is in addition to the pre-admissibility step to the refugee status determination (RSD) process, which has created additional delays. Asylum seekers pending RSD can wait up to a year for a decision. UNHCR has highlighted a deteriorating protection environment in Ecuador for refugees, citing delays in registration, revocations of refugee status, labor exploitation, a more active presence of illegal armed groups and criminal gangs, forced recruitment of minors, and increasing xenophobia and discrimination. Other countries in the region, such as Costa Rica, Venezuela, the Dominican Republic, and Panama, also have established asylum procedures, but the registration and determination procedures are often implemented ineffectively. UNHCR is working with these countries, including Ecuador, to improve their asylum processes.

In Panama, many of the 1,725 recognized refugees and 15,000 persons of concern are Colombians. After more than a decade of ineffective handling of the temporary humanitarian protection status holders (PTH) situation, Panama's Office for Assistance to Refugees (ONPAR) delivered permanent resident documentation to 200 PTH holders in March and 213 will receive it later this year. In Costa Rica, there are 12,737 recognized refugees and 8,290 of persons of concern to UNHCR. Under a new migration law, Costa Rica re-established its

Refugee Department in March 2010, along with a Migration Tribunal that opened in 2011. The recognition rate for asylum applications is approximately 7.5%. Decisions in asylum cases in Costa Rica can take up to a year yet asylum seekers have the right to work while they are waiting for a decision. There are 4,340 recognized refugees in Venezuela, and UNHCR estimates there are more than 200,000 persons live in a refugee-like situation in the country. In Brazil, there are over 4,000 recognized refugees from 75 countries; the largest numbers are from Angola and Colombia.

Honduras, El Salvador, and Guatemala have in recent years been increasingly impacted by the actions of illegal armed groups, including organized crime, leading to high rates of drug and human trafficking, brutal homicides, and sexual and gender-based violence, among other challenges. This increased violence has contributed to a spike in unaccompanied minors arriving in the United States, from around 6,000 in FY 2010 to some 53,000 in the first three quarters of FY 2014. According to UNHCR, the number of people from these three countries seeking asylum in Belize, Costa Rica, Mexico, Nicaragua, and Panama increased by more than seven times between 2008 and 2013.

Religious Freedom

In Latin America and the Caribbean, religious freedom is widely recognized and supported by government and society, though there are cases of religious intolerance. In some isolated instances, Christian groups, mainly Evangelicals, Protestants, and Mormons have reported impediments or complications to their practice of religion, establishment of religious institutions, and importation of religious materials. In some areas, there is harassment of Muslims, anti-Muslim cartoons and speech, and marginalization of Afro and indigenous religions. In Cuba, significant government restrictions remain in place.

Although the constitution protects religious freedom, the Government of Cuba continues to monitor aspects of religious life, including interference in church affairs, surveillance of religious institutions, and harassment of outspoken church leaders. The U.S. Refugee Admissions Program in Havana offers Cubans who have been persecuted on a number of grounds, including their religious beliefs, the opportunity for permanent resettlement in the United States.

Manifestations of anti-Semitism that occurred throughout the hemisphere at times appeared correlated to the unfolding transitions to democracy in other parts of the world. In Venezuela, anti-Semitism is a growing concern, including instances of anti-Semitism in the government-controlled media.

Voluntary Repatriation

Given the threats and violence in Colombia from illegal armed groups (non-state actors) and the lack of state presence to provide full protection in some areas, UNHCR has not been actively promoting repatriation of Colombian refugees.

Local Integration

The Governments of Costa Rica, Ecuador, Panama, and Venezuela have maintained policies that theoretically allow Colombians in need of protection to obtain asylum and integrate locally, although the processes involved are usually slow and cumbersome. The governments' capacity to review applications and confer refugee status remains limited. Even registered refugees with the right to work in these countries struggle to find stable employment or income opportunities, competing with the large number of poor in host communities. Colombians seeking international protection face high levels of discrimination and xenophobia, and the ability to locally integrate in some areas is difficult. Furthermore, refugees do not live in camps, but rather the large majority live in urban areas. Some Colombian persons of concern (including refugees and asylum seekers) in Ecuador, Costa Rica, Panama, and Venezuela continue to experience harassment by persons associated with armed Colombian groups operating in these countries. Security remains a major concern for the Government of Panama, and Panamanians often equate refugees with drug trafficking and crime.

The Department of State is currently supporting UNHCR's efforts to assist the Dominican Republic and other Caribbean countries in developing systems for conducting refugee status determinations for asylum seekers, including Haitians. The opening of a UNHCR office in the Dominican Republic in 2010 and the agency's continued presence in Haiti have contributed greatly to its ability to address the protection needs of refugees, asylum-seekers, and displaced and stateless persons in mixed migration flows throughout the region. In June 2012, the Dominican Republic's refugee eligibility committee (CONARE) first met. Prior to this meeting, the CONARE had not made a decision on an asylum claim since 2005 and had not made more than 20 decisions since UNHCR handed over responsibility for refugee status determinations to the government in 1997. Since the 2012 meeting CONARE remains paralyzed with only a few cases adjudicated. All cases have been rejected.

Third and In-Country Resettlement

In the past, local integration had been the solution best suited to regional refugee problems in Latin America. In recent years, however, third-country resettlement has become an important alternative for those who face physical risks and have urgent protection needs. Canada, New Zealand, Sweden, Denmark, Norway, and the United States offer resettlement to at-risk Colombian refugees. Currently, the United States accepts referrals from UNHCR and embassies in the region and processes these cases principally in Ecuador, with occasional cases in Costa Rica and other countries throughout the region. Under the "Solidarity Resettlement Program," a component of the Mexico Plan of Action which sought regional solutions to the Colombian refugee issue, countries in the region including Argentina, Brazil, Chile, and Uruguay are working with UNHCR to resettle a modest number of Colombian refugees. The Department of State is providing technical support to bolster Uruguay's resettlement program. The United States also facilitates the resettlement to third countries of persons interdicted by the U.S. Coast Guard or who enter Guantanamo Naval Station directly and are found by DHS/USCIS to have a well-founded fear of persecution or to be more likely than not to face torture if repatriated to their country of origin. From 1996 to date, approximately 400 such protected persons have been resettled to 20 countries worldwide.

The U.S. government operates an in-country refugee resettlement program in Cuba. The number of persons seeking refugee resettlement remains high, although the backlog of cases pending review by the Department of State for access to the USRAP has been significantly reduced. This backlog of cases contains a shrinking pool of qualified applicants and an increasing rate of fraudulent applications; as such, an unknown number are likely ineligible for the program. Additional Department of State resources are being applied to address the backlogged cases, and we expect the backlog will continue to decrease for cases seeking access to the program by the end of FY 2015. Recent upgrades to the Refugee Annex have been completed, thus allowing the Mission to expand Cultural Orientation classes for approved U.S.-bound applicants. Some approved refugees do not have sufficient funds to pay for the medical exams and passports needed to depart Cuba, delaying their departure. The exit permit requirement was abolished on January 14, 2013. The Refugee Section has not received any recent information regarding individuals who have been prevented by the Cuban government from traveling.

Cubans eligible to apply for admission to the United States through the in-country program include the following:

1. Former political prisoners;
2. Active members of persecuted religious minorities;
3. Human rights activists, long-standing members;
4. Forced labor conscripts (1965-68); and
5. Persons deprived of their professional credentials or subjected to other disproportionately harsh or discriminatory treatment resulting from their perceived or actual political or religious beliefs.

The U.S. government plans to launch in-country refugee programs in Honduras, El Salvador, and Guatemala for unmarried children under 21 of certain lawfully present qualifying relatives residing in the United States. Decisions on several program parameters are still being considered by the Departments of State and Homeland Security and will be briefed to Congress before the program is implemented.

FY 2014 U.S. Admissions

We anticipate admitting more than 4,000 refugees from Latin America and the Caribbean during FY 2014. Cubans compose the overwhelming majority of refugees resettled from the region. Historically, most Cuban admissions were former political prisoners and forced labor conscripts. The program was expanded in 1991 to include human rights activists, displaced professionals, and others with claims of persecution, which currently compose the majority of admissions. We expect about 500 Colombian refugees to be admitted to the United States during FY 2014.

FY 2015 U.S. Resettlement Program

The proposed 4,000 ceiling for Latin America and the Caribbean for FY 2015 comprises Cuban refugees eligible for the in-country Priority 2 program; a small number of UNHCR-referred Priority 1 Colombians; as well as a small number of Priority 3 family reunification cases. Depending on when the in-country P-2 program for minors in Central America is launched, a small number might be admitted in late FY 2015.

Proposed FY 2015 Latin America program to include arrivals from the following categories:

Priority 1 Individual Referrals	***700***
Priority 2*	***3,250***
Priority 3 Family Reunification	***<u>50</u>***
Total Proposed Ceiling	***4,000***
*to include in-country Cubans and in-country minors in Honduras, El Salvador, and Guatemala.	

NEAR EAST AND SOUTH ASIA

The Near East/South Asia region remains host to more than eight million refugees, primarily Afghans, Bhutanese, Iranians, Iraqis, Palestinians, Sri Lankans, Tibetans, and now Syrians. Few countries in the region are party to the 1951 Convention relating to the Status of Refugees and/or its 1967 Protocol. Nonetheless, many host governments tolerate the presence of refugees within their borders.

UNHCR, ICRC, IOM, WFP, UNRWA, and other humanitarian organizations work with refugees in the region. Some countries have provided long-term protection and/or asylum, mainly to Tibetans, Bhutanese, Sri Lankans, Palestinians, Afghans, Somalis, Syrians, and a handful of other nationalities. Refugees identified by UNHCR for third-country resettlement include Iraqis in Jordan, Syria, Turkey, Lebanon, Egypt, Yemen, and the Gulf States; Bhutanese in Nepal; Afghans in Pakistan, Iran, Turkey, Syria, and India; and Iranians in Turkey. In 2014, UNHCR also began to refer several thousand vulnerable Syrian refugees residing in Turkey, Lebanon, Jordan, Iraq and Egypt to a number of resettlement countries.

As of February 28, 2014, 88,991 Iraqi refugees were registered with UNHCR in the region. There is no internationally agreed-upon number of Iraqi refugees and internally displaced persons due to the fact that not all are registered with UNHCR and they are dispersed throughout the region. UNHCR reports that approximately 950,000 Iraqis displaced by sectarian violence following the Samarra Mosque bombing of February 2006 remain internally displaced, and the Government of Iraq's Ministry of Migration and Displacement reports that an additional 440,000 Iraqis have been displaced since January 2014 by violence in

Anbar province. As of March 30, 2014, there were 219,579 Syrian refugees in Iraq, as well as approximately 36,000 refugees and 6,500 asylum seekers of other origins (including Palestinians and Iranian Kurds).

Intense fighting in Syria has caused massive displacement, both internally and to countries in the region. As of April 15, 2014, there were approximately 2.7 million Syrian refugees in Lebanon, Jordan, Turkey, Iraq, and Egypt. The U.S. government is providing humanitarian assistance to refugees from Syria throughout the region through support to international organizations, such as UNHCR, UNICEF, UNRWA, UNFPA, IOM, ICRC, and WFP, as well as through non-governmental organizations, which are providing critical assistance such as water and sanitation, shelter, and medical care. As of April 24, 2014, the U.S. government had provided more than $1.7 billion in critical humanitarian assistance.

Despite the voluntary repatriation of over 5.8 million Afghan refugees since 2002, Pakistan and Iran continue to host, respectively, approximately 1.6 million and 800,000 registered Afghans, many of whom have resided in these countries for decades. The maintenance of asylum and protection space for those refugees who cannot yet return to Afghanistan while continuing to support voluntary repatriation, is a top priority for the U.S. government and for UNHCR. In addition to Afghan refugees, some 2-3 million Afghans are believed to live and work in Pakistan and Iran as economic migrants without documentation. There are more than 27,000 registered Afghan asylum-seekers in Turkey and an estimated 40,000 total (registered and unregistered), many of whom fled from Iran. Over 11,000 Afghan refugees and asylum seekers are also registered with UNHCR in India. Identifying durable solutions remains an important component of UNHCR's strategy in India. Local integration in South Asia remains a difficult option due to opposition from host countries.

Thousands of ethnic Nepalis in Bhutan were forced out of Bhutan in the early 1990s as a result of the Bhutanese government's policy of "one nation and one people" (also referred to as "Bhutanization"). Despite 17 rounds of formal negotiations between Bhutan and Nepal, and pressure from the United States and other governments to resolve the issue and secure the right of return for genuine Bhutanese nationals, particularly humanitarian cases, to date none have been permitted to return. Due to concerted resettlement efforts commenced in late 2007 by the United States and other resettlement countries, approximately 90,000 of the original population of 108,000 Bhutanese refugees in Nepal have departed after spending two decades in camps in eastern Nepal. The U.S. government continues to press the Government of Bhutan to help resolve this protracted situation by accepting the return of eligible refugees who wish to repatriate. Similarly, the U.S. government encourages the Government of Nepal to allow local integration of the remaining refugees.

Religious Freedom

Persecution of religious groups is common in many countries in the Middle East and South Asia that are countries of origin for refugee populations entering the United States. State and local government responses to violence against members of religious groups, particularly Muslims and Christians, are often inadequate. Although many of these countries do not have Jewish populations, anti-Semitism is prevalent, and often espoused by governments or religious leaders, especially in Iran.

In Afghanistan, religious freedom is limited due to constitutional contradictions, legislative ambiguity, and interpretations of Islamic law that punish apostasy and blasphemy.

In Pakistan, the penal code includes blasphemy laws that carry punishments ranging from imprisonment to the death penalty. Frequent abuses of these laws negatively affect religious minorities, both Muslims and non-Muslims. In 2013, 34 new cases were registered under the blasphemy law, and 18 Ahmadis were arrested in matters related to their faith, though at least one death sentence for blasphemy was overturned, and the government has yet to carry out a death sentence for blasphemy. Nevertheless, at least 17 people are awaiting execution for blasphemy, and at least 20 others are serving life sentences.

In Sri Lanka, religious tensions continue to be a problem, and Muslim, Hindu, and Buddhist communities often distrust one another. In 2013, local authorities failed to respond effectively to communal violence, including attacks on members of minority religious groups, and perpetrators were not brought to justice. Authorities failed to prevent the destruction of a Hindu temple in Dambulla and an attack on the Grandpass Mosque in Colombo. Nongovernmental organizations alleged that senior and local government officials provided assistance to or, at a minimum, tacit support for the actions of societal groups targeting religious minorities.

In Bhutan, Buddhism is the state's "spiritual heritage," although in the southern areas many citizens openly practice Hinduism. While subtle pressure on non-Buddhists to observe the traditional Buddhist values and some limitations on constructing non-Buddhist religious buildings remain, the government has taken steps to improve religious freedom in the country. Some societal pressures toward non-Buddhists are reflected in official and unofficial efforts to uphold the "spiritual heritage" (Buddhism) of the country.

In Iran, religious groups, including Sunni Muslims, Baha'is, Sufis, Jews, Zoroastrians, Yaresanis, and Christians, continue to face official discrimination, harassment, and arrest. Members of the Shia community who express religious views different from those of the government are also subject to harassment and intimidation. The government continues convictions and executions of dissidents, political reformists, and peaceful protesters on the charge of moharebeh (enmity against God) and anti-Islamic propaganda.

Increasing sectarian violence, while generally centered around Sunni-Shia divisions, impacts all of Iraq's religious communities. Iraq's minority communities, including Christians, Yezidis, Sabean-Mandaeans, and others, have experienced wide-scale displacement. Some 20 percent of registered Iraqi refugees are members of religious minorities, a figure appreciably larger than their percentage of the overall Iraqi population. As a result, some of these religious communities, along with their ancient languages and customs, are on the verge of disappearing.

In Syria, the government increased its targeting and surveillance of members of faith groups it deemed a "threat," including members of the country's Sunni majority. This occurred concurrently with the escalation of violent extremist activity targeting Christians and other religious minorities as the current civil war continues. Large-scale internal and external displacement of all sectors of the population was ongoing.

In Egypt, the government generally failed to prevent, investigate, or prosecute crimes against members of religious minority groups, especially Coptic Christians – including the recent attack at the Cathedral of St. Mark, the seat of the Coptic Orthodox Pope. This fostered a culture of impunity. Christians, Shias, Bahais, and other minorities faced personal and collective discrimination, especially in government employment and the ability to build, renovate, and repair places of worship. The government routinely failed to condemn and sometimes contributed to incendiary speech, including anti-Semitic, anti-Christian, and anti-Shia speech.

In some countries in the region, most notably Afghanistan, Iran, Saudi Arabia, Pakistan, and Egypt, blasphemy, apostasy, and defamation of religion laws are used to restrict religious liberty, constrain the rights of religious minorities, and limit freedom of expression, and those accused face threats of violence. Under these governments' interpretations of Islamic law, individuals have their civil rights infringed upon if any member of society files a complaint against them. In most countries in the region Sharia courts decide personal status cases. Iran and Saudi Arabia are designated by the Department of State as CPCs under the International Religious Freedom Act of 1998 for systematic, ongoing, and egregious violations of religious freedom.

The USRAP provides resettlement access in various ways to refugees who suffer religious persecution. Under the Specter Amendment, Iranian religious minorities designated as Priority 2 category members are considered under a reduced evidentiary standard for establishing a well-founded fear of persecution. Iranian refugees have also gained access to the program through Priority 3. In addition, the USRAP accepts UNHCR and embassy referrals of religious minorities of various nationalities in the region. Nationals of any country, including CPCs, may be referred to the U.S. program by UNHCR or a U.S. embassy for reasons of religious persecution.

Voluntary Repatriation

After the fall of the Taliban in 2001, voluntary repatriation to Afghanistan proceeded on a massive scale for several years, both with and without UNHCR assistance. Since 2002, over 5.8 million Afghan refugees have returned, mostly from Pakistan and Iran. Over 4.7 million have been assisted by UNHCR in the largest repatriation operation in UNHCR's history. However, the era of mass returns has largely ended, with about 39,000 returning in 2013. The substantial repatriation represents roughly 20 percent of Afghanistan's total population and has taxed the country's capacity to absorb them, let alone additional refugee returns.

It is unlikely that all of the remaining 2.4 million registered Afghans in Pakistan and Iran will repatriate. UNHCR and IOM's assessment is that the continuing migration of Afghans in both directions across the Afghanistan-Pakistan border is part of a larger process of economic and social migration that has been occurring for centuries. UNHCR is working with the Governments of Afghanistan, Pakistan, and Iran and the international community to develop policies and programs to sustain voluntary returns. They are also working to better manage the residual Afghan population in Pakistan by working toward longer-term protection and migration solutions. IOM is seeking a greater role in border management and in developing regional mechanisms for economic migration that would bolster protection for Afghans. The Government of the Islamic Republic of Afghanistan is working to increase its capacity in helping returnees fold back into Afghan economic and social structures and at the same time prioritizes continued protection for Afghan citizens still seeking refuge abroad. UNHCR, together with the Governments of Afghanistan, Iran, and Pakistan, continue to work toward implementing the *Solutions Strategy for*

Afghan Refugees to Support Voluntary Repatriation, Sustainable Reintegration and Assistance to Host Countries (SSAR). The SSAR provides for the orderly, voluntary return of Afghan refugees and emphasizes the need to reintegrate returned refugees into their communities fully.

Stabilizing the displaced Afghan population – e.g., reintegrating returning refugees and IDPs into Afghan society and preserving asylum space for refugees in neighboring countries – is critical to regional stability, as is addressing irregular migration. Through a unique quadripartite consultative process, UNHCR and the Governments of Afghanistan, Iran, and Pakistan have agreed on a multi-year regional strategy, endorsed by the international community in May 2012 to address assistance to Afghan refugees and returnees, emphasizing cross-border linkages. The Afghan government has also adopted a national IDP policy which seeks to address protection, assistance, and durable solutions issues for displaced populations within its borders. With assistance from UNHCR and others, the Afghan government plans to begin implementing the IDP policy in 2015.

Since 2008, more than 1.2 million IDPs and refugees have returned to their homes in Iraq, with IDPs comprising 76 percent of these returns. About 81 percent of all returns have been to Baghdad and Diyala, a province northeast of Baghdad. This trend generally matches displacement patterns as over 80 percent of all the pre-2014 IDPs and 70 percent of all refugees were displaced from those locations. UNHCR will assist Iraqis in neighboring countries wishing to return to Iraq by facilitating voluntary return, but it is not encouraging returns at this time. In 2012, nearly 85,000 Iraqi refugees, approximately 56,500 of whom were living in Syria, returned to Iraq and registered for assistance through the Iraqi government or UNHCR. UNHCR reported no voluntary repatriations of Iraqis from Syria between January and July 2013 and only limited voluntary repatriations, 1,281 individuals, from other countries in the region during the same time period.

The United States continues to work with other interested governments in urging the Government of Bhutan to allow for the voluntary repatriation of Bhutanese refugees to Bhutan under acceptable terms and conditions. With the end of the conflict in Sri Lanka, approximately 12,000 refugees have returned. However, the number of Tamils seeking to return from India has decreased. So far in 2014, UNHCR assisted in the voluntary return of 111 Tamil refugees to Sri Lanka.

Local Integration

The SSAR promotes enhancing support for refugee-hosting communities and providing some alternative stay arrangements for refugees in Afghanistan and Iran. While some progress is being made, few countries in the region offer local integration to refugees. In July 2013, the Government of Pakistan endorsed the policies found in the *National Policy on Management and Repatriation of Afghan Refugees beyond 30th June, 2013*. At the same meeting, the Cabinet extended the validity of Afghan Proof of Registration cards and the Tripartite Agreement (among the governments of Afghanistan and Pakistan and UNHCR) until December 31, 2015. As part of the Pakistan implementation of the SSAR and in partnership with the Government of Pakistan and UN agencies, UNHCR launched the Refugee-Affected and Hosting Areas (RAHA) initiative in 2009. This program is widely regarded as a success in addressing Afghan refugee and Pakistani host community needs by rehabilitating areas that have been adversely affected by the presence of Afghan refugee communities over the past 30 years. The United States will continue to work with UNHCR and the Government of Pakistan to preserve asylum space and promote alternative stay arrangements. However, at present, local integration is not an option for most of the Afghan refugees.

Syria hosted more than 29,000 UNHCR-registered Iraqi refugees as of January 31, 2014. Iraqis do not need a visa to enter Syria. They receive a stamp upon entry, which allows for six months of residence and should be renewed at the local government offices. Because of the continuing violence in Syria, many Iraqis have fled the country. The Government of Jordan (GOJ) requires visas for Iraqis and has instituted an additional visa category for Iraqis coming to Jordan from Syria since unrest broke out in Syria in 2011. The GOJ continues to preserve first asylum and protection space for Iraqi refugees and remains a generous host.

Iraqis in Syria and Jordan are not legally defined as refugees, but rather as guests. Both governments allow UNHCR to register Iraqis. With help from the international community, the Governments of Syria and Jordan have allowed Iraqi students to enroll in public schools. However, enrollments in both countries have been lower than anticipated. In both Syria and Jordan, Iraqi refugees have access to the public health care systems. Although the Government of Jordan has granted access to several legal labor sectors to Iraqis, few have obtained work permits as they are also required to obtain residency permits, which the GOJ is not issuing to Iraqis. Iraqis do not have access to the legal labor market in Syria.

The Government of Iraq has acknowledged that many Iraqi IDPs will not be able to return to their home communities, and instead require support integrating into their areas of displacement. UNHCR and other international partners are also seeking to support local integration as a viable option for IDPs, but they point out that, in addition to the integration grant, it will be important for displaced Iraqis to be able to access services in their areas of displacement.

While Turkey ratified the 1951 UN Refugee Convention and acceded to its 1967 Protocol, the Turkish government acceded to the Protocol with a geographic limitation acknowledging refugees only from Europe. While most asylum seekers are thus not considered refugees under Turkish law, the Turkish government grants temporary refuge and temporary local integration possibilities to refugees recognized by UNHCR usually pending their referral to a potential resettlement country. As of January 31, 2014, there were more than 40,000 persons registered with UNHCR Turkey, the majority from Iraq (42%), Afghanistan (24%) and Iran (20%). In addition to the Syrian influx into Turkey over the past year, Turkey has also seen substantial, increased arrivals of Iraqis due to the increased violence in neighboring Iraq. UNHCR-recognized refugees and asylum seekers in Turkey are assigned to one of 64 satellite cities. Provincial governments are responsible for meeting their basic needs, including by providing access to employment, healthcare, and education although support varies from one location to another. On April 4, 2013, the Turkish Parliament passed the "Foreigners and International Protection Law," which will regulate the entry, exit, and the stay of migrants in the country, along with the scope of international protection for those who seek asylum in Turkey. The law went into full implementation on April 11, 2014.

Despite the increasing number of asylum seekers and refugees, India does not have a clear national policy for the treatment of refugees, and UNHCR has a limited mandate in the country. In New Delhi, urban refugees face difficult conditions, including discrimination and harassment by the local population, limiting their local integration prospects. India permits UNHCR to assist urban refugees in New Delhi, primarily Burmese, Afghans, and Somalis. India recognizes and aids certain groups, including Sri Lankan Tamils and Tibetans in the 112 camps for Sri Lankans and 39 settlements for Tibetans located throughout the country. The Government of India provides support and benefits to registered Tibetan and Sri Lankan refugees. It also grants work authorization to documented Tibetans. However, Sri Lankan refugees in India do not receive work authorization from the central government but are unofficially allowed to work on the informal economy.

UNHCR has negotiated an agreement with the Government of India whereby India would facilitate access to citizenship for Hindu and Sikh Afghan refugees who meet the standard criteria to acquire Indian citizenship, while UNHCR would pursue resettlement opportunities for other long-staying ethnic Afghan refugees. Naturalization clinics were established to support the citizenship process for Hindu and Sikh Afghans, and UNHCR intensified its efforts to ensure that all eligible refugees had submitted applications for Indian citizenship by December 31, 2009. As a result, over 4,400 applications were submitted and over 680 Afghans have naturalized.

Third-Country Resettlement

The USRAP anticipates the continued large-scale processing of Iraqis, and, to a lesser extent, Bhutanese and Iranians, and the launch of significant processing of Syrians during FY 2015. As of mid-June 2014, RSC pre-screening and USCIS adjudications in Baghdad were suspended due to the relocation of personnel outside Iraq. It is unclear when they will resume. Applicants who were approved by USCIS prior to the suspension continue to depart as security and medical checks are cleared.

In late 2013, UNHCR announced its intention to refer 30,000 Syrian refugees for resettlement in third countries by the end of 2014 and up to 100,000 additional Syrian refugees by 2016. The United States will play a significant role in this effort. The majority of Syrian referrals will be processed in Turkey, Jordan, Lebanon, and to a lesser extent in Egypt, and the Iraqi Kurdistan Region. As of August 2014, UNHCR had referred some 2,500 Syrians for U.S. resettlement consideration and we expect this number to rise dramatically in the second half of the year, including individuals with close family ties in the U.S. Those who are approved will begin to arrive in FY 2015.

The United States recognizes that the possibility of third-country resettlement must be available to the most vulnerable Iraqi refugees, and has processing facilities in Amman, Baghdad, Beirut, Cairo, Damascus, and Istanbul. While many Iraqis gain access to the USRAP via a referral from UNHCR, we are also facilitating direct access to the USRAP for Iraqis with close U.S. affiliations in a limited number of countries in the region. The Refugee Crisis in Iraq Act, enacted January 28, 2008, created categories of Iraqis who are eligible for direct access (P-2) to the USRAP, both inside and outside Iraq. Currently, beneficiaries of P-2 categories who may seek access to the USRAP in Jordan, Egypt, Iraq, and the UAE include:

1. Iraqis who work/worked on a full-time basis as interpreters/translators for the U.S. Government, MNF-I in Iraq, or U.S. Forces-Iraq;
2. Iraqis who are/were employed by the U.S. Government in Iraq;
3. Iraqis who are/were employees of an organization or entity closely associated with the U.S. mission in Iraq that has received U.S. Government funding through an official and documented contract, award, grant or cooperative agreement;
4. Iraqis who are/were employed in Iraq by a U.S.-based media organization or non-governmental organization;
5. Spouses, sons, daughters, parents, and siblings of individuals described in the four categories above, or of an individual eligible for a Special Immigrant Visa as a result of his/her employment by or on behalf of the U.S. Government in Iraq, including if the individual is no longer alive, provided that the relationship is verified; and
6. Iraqis who are the spouses, sons, daughters, parents, brothers, or sisters of a citizen of the United States, or who are the spouses or unmarried sons or daughters of a Permanent Resident Alien of the United States, as established by their being or becoming beneficiaries of approved family-based I-130 Immigrant Visa Petitions.

The United States has increased its in-country processing capacity nearly 300 percent since establishing a Resettlement Support Center in Baghdad in FY 2008. Although security and logistical challenges associated with operating an RSC in Iraq limit in-country processing capacity, refugee admissions from Iraq are exceeding those from neighboring countries. Refugee processing in Iraq is a high priority for the United States as it directly benefits Iraqis associated with U.S. efforts in Iraq. DHS continues to devote substantial resources to Iraqi refugee processing and maintains a robust interview schedule in the region, except in Iraq, as of June 2014.

Middle Eastern and South Asian refugees in most of Europe avail themselves of the asylum systems of the countries in which they are located. In Vienna, however, certain Iranian religious minorities (Baha'is, Zoroastrians, Jews, Mandaeans, and Christians) may be processed for U.S. resettlement using special procedures authorized by the Government of Austria. The Lautenberg legislation expired in September 2012 and was subsequently re-authorized in March 2013, allowing new applications to be filed and adjudicated under Lautenberg guidelines. The United States also processes Iranian religious minorities (primarily Baha'i) and other Iranians in Turkey through special procedures involving fast-track refugee status determination and referral by UNHCR.

Resettlement processing for Bhutanese refugees in Nepal is continuing smoothly and the United States remains committed to considering for resettlement as many refugees as have expressed interest. As of June 2014, UNHCR had referred over 105,000 Bhutanese refugees for resettlement to eight countries and more than 90,000 of these Bhutanese refugees have been resettled to these countries – most notably the United States – since late 2007. In April 2014, UNHCR and eight other participating resettlement countries requested that all Bhutanese refugees who were interested in resettlement declare their interest to UNHCR by June 30, 2014. This deadline allowed UNHCR and donor countries to better understand resource needs for the final phase of the resettlement program and continued assistance to the residual population that will remain in Nepal. Processing of Bhutanese refugees who have declared interest in resettlement will take several more years.

The United States works with Australia and other countries to preserve protection space and to coordinate the resettlement of Afghans from Pakistan; we anticipate overall increased UNHCR referrals in coming years with a larger percentage being directed to the United States. In India, UNHCR currently refers some 400 individuals per year, with priority given to those they deem most vulnerable. The majority of referrals are Burmese. UNHCR also refers a very limited number of refugees out of Sri Lanka, mostly Pakistanis. We continue to explore modalities for processing vulnerable Tibetan refugees in the region.

FY 2014 U.S. Admissions

We estimate the admission of approximately 34,000 refugees from the region in FY 2014. These will include some 9,000 Bhutanese, 19,000 Iraqis, 3,000 Iranians, and several hundred Afghans, including women who had been living in Iran processed through the UNHCR Emergency Transit Center in Slovakia.

FY 2015 U.S. Resettlement Program

The proposed regional ceiling for refugees from the Near East and South Asia for FY 2015 is 33,000, including vulnerable Iraqis, Bhutanese, Iranians, Syrians, Pakistanis, and Afghans. We expect individual UNHCR referrals of various religious and ethnic groups in the region, including Assyrians, Mandeans, Iranian Kurds, and Syrian Kurds. In addition, Ahmadi Muslims in many locations and Afghans in the former Soviet Union, Pakistan, India, and elsewhere will be included.

Proposed FY 2015 Near East/ South Asia program to include arrivals from the following categories:

Priority 1 Individual Referrals	*18,450*
Priority 2 Groups	*14,500*
Priority 3 Family Reunification	*50*
Total Proposed Ceiling	*33,000*

In FY 2013, the USRAP admitted 69,926 refugees from 53 countries. More than half were originally from either Iraq or Burma. (See Table III.)

The demographic characteristics of refugee arrivals from the 20 largest source countries (representing 100 percent of total arrivals) in FY 2013 illustrate the variation among refugee groups. The median age of all FY 2013 arrivals was 25 years and ranged from 19 years for arrivals from the Democratic Republic of Congo, Central African Republic, and Burundi to 35 years of age for arrivals from Cuba and Iran. In FY 2013, 45.95 percent of all arriving refugees were female and 54.05 percent of all arriving refugees were male. Males predominated among refugees from Sudan (79.5 percent), Eritrea (59.9 percent), and Pakistan (57.5 percent). (See Table IV.)

Of the total arrivals in FY 2013, some 9.2 percent were under the age of five, 24.5 percent were of school age, 66.2 percent were of working age, and 3.4 percent were of retirement age. (See Table V.) Considerable variation among refugee groups can be seen among specific age categories. Refugees under the age of five ranged from a high of 13.8 percent among Central African Republic arrivals to a low of 2.4 percent of those from Iran. The number of school-aged children (from five to 17 years of age) varied from a high of over 43.5 percent of arrivals from Burundi to a low of 11.3 percent of those from Iran. The number of working-aged refugees (16 to 64 years of age) varied from a high of 78.8 percent of those from Iran to a low of 46.5 percent of individuals from the Central African Republic. Retirement-aged refugees (65 years or older) ranged from a high of 9.4 percent of arrivals from the Former Soviet Union to a low of less than one percent of those from Burundi.

During FY 2013, 63 percent of all arriving refugees resettled in 12 states. The majority were placed in Texas (10.7 percent), followed by California (9.1 percent), Michigan (6.6 percent), New York (5.7 percent), Florida (5.2 percent), and Arizona (4.4 percent). The states of Ohio (4.0 percent), Georgia (3.9 percent), Pennsylvania (3.6 percent), Illinois (3.5 percent), Washington (3.4 percent), and North Carolina (3.4 percent) also were in the top twelve states where refugees were resettled. (See Table VI.)

TABLE III
Refugee Arrivals By Country of Origin
Fiscal Year 2013

Country of Origin	Arrival Number	% of Total
Afghanistan	661	0.95%
Angola	6	0.01%
Bangladesh	1	0.00%
Bhutan	9,134	13.06%
Bulgaria	1	0.00%
Burma	16,299	23.31%
Burundi	193	0.28%
Cambodia	30	0.04%
Canada	1	0.00%
Central African Republic	318	0.45%
Chad	32	0.05%
China	86	0.12%
Colombia	230	0.33%
Congo	161	0.23%
Cuba	4,205	6.01%
Dem. Rep. Congo	2,563	3.67%
Egypt	3	0.00%
Eritrea	1,824	2.61%
Ethiopia	765	1.09%
Former Soviet Union*	579	0.83%
Gambia	11	0.02%
Guinea	9	0.01%
India	3	0.00%
Iran	2,578	3.69%
Iraq	19,488	27.87%
Ivory Coast	20	0.03%

Jordan	13	0.02%
Kenya	5	0.01%
Korea, North	17	0.02%
Kuwait	12	0.02%
Liberia	94	0.13%
Libya	1	0.00%
Mali	2	0.00%
Nepal	34	0.05%
Nigeria	2	0.00%
Pakistan	158	0.23%
Palestine	164	0.23%
Republic of South Sudan	17	0.02%
Rwanda	139	0.20%
Senegal	2	0.00%
Sierra Leone	4	0.01%
Somalia	7,608	10.88%
Sri Lanka (Ceylon)	92	0.13%
Sudan	2,160	3.09%
Syria	36	0.05%
Thailand	4	0.01%
Tibet	15	0.02%
Togo	18	0.03%
Uganda	15	0.02%
Venezuela	3	0.00%
Vietnam	86	0.12%
Yemen	12	0.02%
Zimbabwe	12	0.02%
TOTAL	**69,926**	**100.00%**

Source: Department of State, Bureau of Population, Refugees, and Migration, Refugee Processing Center

TABLE IV

Median Age and Gender of Refugee Arrivals, Fiscal Year 2013

Rank (# of Arrivals)	Country of Origin	Refugees Admitted	Median Age	% Females	% Males
1	Iraq	19,488	28	47.19%	52.81%
2	Burma	16,299	23	43.95%	56.05%
3	Bhutan	9,134	28	49.09%	50.91%
4	Somalia	7,608	22	45.87%	54.13%
5	Cuba	4,205	35	48.51%	51.49%
6	Iran	2,578	35	48.10%	51.90%
7	Dem. Rep. Congo	2,563	19	50.80%	49.20%
8	Sudan	2,160	27	24.44%	75.56%
9	Eritrea	1,824	23	40.02%	59.98%
10	Ethiopia	765	23	45.88%	54.12%
11	Afghanistan	661	23	46.29%	53.71%
12	Former Soviet Union*	579	30	51.12%	48.88%
13	Central African Republic	318	19	45.60%	54.40%
14	Colombia	230	21	50.43%	49.57%
15	Burundi	193	19	51.81%	48.19%
16	Palestine	164	27	51.22%	48.78%
17	Congo	161	25	48.45%	51.55%
18	Pakistan	158	25	42.41%	57.59%
19	Rwanda	139	23	60.43%	39.57%
20	Liberia	94	23	54.26%	45.74%
21	All Other Countries	605	27	45.45%	54.55%
TOTAL		**69,926**	**25**	**45.94%**	**54.06%**

Source: Department of State, Bureau of Population, Refugees, and Migration, Refugee Processing Center

TABLE V

Select Age Categories of Refugee Arrivals, Fiscal Year 2013

Rank (# of Arrivals)	Country of Origin	Under 5 Yrs	School Age (5-17)	Working Age (16-64)	Retirement Age (=or > 65)
1	Iraq	8.64%	24.07%	65.35%	5.05%
2	Burma	13.34%	23.44%	65.02%	1.37%
3	Bhutan	7.30%	21.89%	69.49%	5.28%
4	Somalia	9.70%	31.56%	62.20%	0.95%
5	Cuba	4.23%	20.74%	72.63%	6.21%
6	Iran	2.44%	11.37%	78.90%	9.23%
7	Dem. Rep. Congo	11.74%	40.73%	53.06%	0.51%
8	Sudan	8.56%	16.57%	76.48%	0.56%
9	Eritrea*	7.68%	24.12%	70.83%	0.44%
10	Ethiopia	13.20%	20.13%	69.15%	0.26%
11	Afghanistan	6.51%	33.59%	64.30%	1.21%
12	Former Soviet Union*	9.15%	25.73%	60.45%	9.50%
13	Central African Republic	13.84%	42.77%	46.54%	0.94%
14	Colombia	8.70%	39.13%	55.65%	0.87%
15	Burundi	12.44%	43.52%	48.19%	0.00%
16	Palestine	9.15%	29.88%	59.15%	5.49%
17	Congo	9.32%	32.92%	60.25%	1.86%
18	Pakistan	7.59%	28.48%	66.46%	0.63%
19	Rwanda	4.32%	36.69%	65.47%	0.72%
20	Liberia	5.32%	39.36%	59.57%	1.06%
21	All Other Countries	4.30%	28.10%	71.40%	1.98%
TOTAL		**9.29%**	**24.54%**	**66.29%**	**3.42%**

NOTE: Totals may exceed 100 percent due to overlapping age categories.

Source: Department of State, Bureau of Population, Refugees, and Migration, Refugee Processing Center

TABLE VI

Refugee Arrivals By State of Initial Resettlement, Fiscal Year 2013

STATE	Refugee Arrivals	Amerasian Arrivals	Total Arrivals	% of Total Arrivals to U.S.
Alabama	129	0	129	0.18%
Alaska	106	0	106	0.15%
Arizona	3,052	0	3,052	4.36%
Arkansas	7	0	7	0.01%
California	6,379	4	6,383	9.13%
Colorado	1,789	0	1,789	2.56%
Connecticut	547	0	547	0.78%
Delaware	6	0	6	0.01%
District of Columbia	11	0	11	0.02%
Florida	3,613	0	3,613	5.17%
Georgia	2,710	0	2,710	3.88%
Hawaii	6	0	6	0.01%
Idaho	920	0	920	1.32%
Illinois	2,453	0	2,453	3.51%
Indiana	1,541	0	1,541	2.20%
Iowa	598	0	598	0.86%
Kansas	474	0	474	0.68%
Kentucky	1,603	0	1,603	2.29%
Louisiana	223	0	223	0.32%
Maine	350	0	350	0.50%
Maryland	1,242	0	1,242	1.78%
Massachusetts	1,829	0	1,829	2.62%
Michigan	4,651	0	4,651	6.65%
Minnesota	2,214	0	2,214	3.17%
Mississippi	3	0	3	0.00%
Missouri	1,268	0	1,268	1.81%
Nebraska	997	0	997	1.43%
Nevada	563	0	563	0.81%
New Hampshire	379	0	379	0.54%
New Jersey	443	0	443	0.63%
New Mexico	293	0	293	0.42%

STATE	Refugee Arrivals	Amerasian Arrivals	Total Arrivals	% of Total Arrivals to U.S.
New York	3,965	0	3,965	5.67%
North Carolina	2,377	0	2,377	3.40%
North Dakota	456	0	456	0.65%
Ohio	2,788	0	2,788	3.99%
Oklahoma	300	0	300	0.43%
Oregon	875	0	875	1.25%
Pennsylvania	2,507	0	2,507	3.59%
Puerto Rico	3	0	3	0.00%
Rhode Island	171	0	171	0.24%
South Carolina	148	0	148	0.21%
South Dakota	533	0	533	0.76%
Tennessee	1,557	0	1,557	2.23%
Texas	7,466	9	7,475	10.69%
Utah	1,189	0	1,189	1.70%
Vermont	322	0	322	0.46%
Virginia	1,472	0	1,472	2.11%
Washington	2,414	0	2,414	3.45%
West Virginia	25	0	25	0.04%
Wisconsin	942	4	946	1.35%
Total	**69,909**	**17**	**69,926**	**100.00%**

Note: Arrival figures do not reflect secondary migration.

Source: Department of State, Bureau of Population, Refugees, and Migration, Refugee Processing Center

TABLE VII

ESTIMATED AVAILABLE FUNDING FOR REFUGEE PROCESSING, MOVEMENT, AND RESETTLEMENT
FY 2014 AND FY 2015 ($ MILLIONS)

AGENCY	ESTIMATED FY 2014 (BY DEPARTMENT)	ESTIMATED FY 2015 (BY DEPARTMENT)
DEPARTMENT OF HOMELAND SECURITY *United States Citizenship and Immigration Services*		
Refugee Processing [1]	$32.3	$32.9
DEPARTMENT OF STATE *Bureau of Population, Refugees, and Migration*		
Refugee Admissions [2,3]	$494.4	$ 418.0
DEPARTMENT OF HEALTH AND HUMAN SERVICES *Administration for Children and Families, Office of Refugee Resettlement*		
Refugee Resettlement [4]	$616.3	$608.1
TOTAL	**$1,143.0**	**$1,059.0**

The estimated FY 2015 figures above reflect the President's FY 2015 Budget request and do not include carryover funds from FY 2014.

[1] FY 2015: Includes cost factors to reflect Headquarters facilities rent related to the refugee resettlement program, projected staffing enhancements, and following-to-join refugee processing, in addition to certain ICASS costs.

[2] FY 2014: Includes FY 2014 MRA appropriation of $351 million, $68.8 million in PRM carryover from FY 2013, $68.6 million projected IOM loan collections/carryover, and an estimate of $6 million in prior year MRA recoveries. A portion of these funds will be carried forward into FY 2015.

[3] FY 2015: Includes FY 2015 MRA budget request of $360 million, $52 million in projected IOM loan collections/carryover, and an estimate of $6 million in prior year MRA recoveries. Funds carried forward from FY 2014 will also be available in FY 2015.

[4] FY 2014 and FY 2015: HHS's Office of Refugee Resettlement's (ORR) refugee benefits and services are also provided to asylees, Cuban and Haitian entrants, certain Amerasians from Vietnam, victims of a severe form of trafficking who have received certification or eligibility letters from ORR, and certain family members who are accompanying or following to join victims of severe forms of trafficking, and some victims of torture, as well as Iraqi and Afghan Special Immigrants and their spouses and unmarried children under the age of 21. None of these additional groups is included in the refugee admissions ceiling except Amerasians. This category does not include costs associated with the Unaccompanied Alien Children's Program, Temporary Assistance for Needy Families (TANF), Medicaid, Supplemental Security Income

programs, or the Victims of Domestic Trafficking. The estimated FY 2015 figures above reflect the President's FY 2015 Budget request and do not include carryover funds from FY 2014, as HHS does not anticipate any carryover funding from FY 2014.

TABLE VIII
UNHCR Resettlement Statistics by Resettlement Country CY 2013 Admissions

RESETTLEMENT COUNTRY	TOTAL	PERCENT OF TOTAL RESETTLED
United States	47,875	67.04%
Australia	11,117	15.57%
Canada	5,140	7.20%
Sweden	1,832	2.57%
Germany	1,092	1.53%
Norway	941	1.32%
United Kingdom	750	1.05%
New Zealand	682	0.96%
Finland	665	0.93%
Denmark	475	0.67%
Netherlands	362	0.51%
Belgium	100	0.14%
France	100	0.14%
Switzerland	78	0.11%
Ireland	62	0.09%
Brazil	56	0.08%
Rep. of Korea	31	0.04%
Japan	18	0.03%
Uruguay	14	0.02%
Argentina	7	0.00%
Portugal	6	0.00%
Austria	4	0.00%
Chile	3	0.00%
Czech. Rep.	1	0.00%
TOTAL	71,411	100.00%

www.ingramcontent.com/pod-product-compliance
Lightning Source LLC
Chambersburg PA
CBHW081410280526
45788CB00009B/3041